CHANA LEVITAN, MSc

THAT'S WHY I MARRIED YOU!

How to Dance with Personality Differences

gefen publishing house

JERUSALEM ◆ NEW YORK   Est. 1981

Cover design: Leah Ben Avraham/Noonim Graphics
Typesetting: Raphaël Freeman, Renana Typesetting

ISBN: 978-965-229-828-7

1 3 5 7 9 8 6 4 2

Gefen Publishing House Ltd.
6 Hatzvi Street
Jerusalem 94386, Israel
+972-2-538-0247
orders@gefenpublishing.com

Gefen Books
11 Edison Place
Springfield, NJ 07081
+1-516-593-1234
orders@gefenpublishing.com

www.gefenpublishing.com   *Send for our free catalog*

Printed in Israel

Contents

Acknowledgments

I am deeply indebted to Sarah Glazer, my right-hand first-draft editor, who graced the first draft of this manuscript with her sheer editorial brilliance and astute comments.

Special thanks to Dr. Sharon Slater and Dr. Mordechai Markson, two therapists par excellence, for their expert advice, feedback, guidance, and encouragement throughout the conception and writing of this book. And a huge thank-you to David Levinstein, MSW, prominent therapist and supervisor, for graciously sharing his invaluable insights and wise suggestions in various sections of my manuscript.

No usual thanks are sufficient to express the depth of my gratitude to my wonderful team of colleagues – and dear friends – for the countless hours they put into my manuscript, from day one of its writing: Tobi Friedman, BS; Dina Kessler, MSc; Lisa Lawrence, MSW; Arona Pokroy, MSc; and Abby Weiss, MSW. Having such a talented and insightful team by my side throughout the process was a true gift.

I am tremendously grateful to Jackie Engel, whose special touch and savvy creativity played an enormous role in the development of this manuscript – and its launch as well. And a massive thank-you to Sara Kohn, whose painstaking scrutiny of this manuscript and spot-on insights contributed immensely to what the book is today.

To a very important colleague of mine who was involved in every page of this book, who is an inspiring thinker and spiritual guide to so many – I cannot thank you enough. This book would not be what it is without your consistent involvement and input. Although you prefer to remain unnamed, you know who you are.

To the esteemed Dr. David Williamson and Dr. Rudy Seward of the University of North Texas, many thanks for the guidance throughout the research of this book. And to my research assistants, Laurie Baron, MSW; Deanne Goldberg-Kawalsky, MA; and Michelle Penn, BA; I extend my gratitude for their gracious assistance with interviews and data. Much appreciation goes to Rabbi Raphael Butler for diving in to assist, amidst his incredibly busy schedule.

To my wonderful, generous colleagues and friends, for their extremely insightful and important comments on my manuscript. Although I list you together, each one of you deserves to be thanked individually: Dini Coopersmith, Marianna Feldman, Lanie Goldenberg, Shelley Hebert, Rikki Jacobson-Davies, Phyllis Jesselson, Liba Markson, Michael Akiva Prell, Jeremy Ravinsky, Danielle Rothman, and Yehoshua Stein.

My gratitude goes to my super proactive publisher at Gefen Publishing, Ilan Greenfield, and senior editor Kezia Raffel Pride, for their immediate excitement and enthusiasm when they "met" my manuscript – and for their continued commitment and dedication throughout. Kezia's expert and superb editorial touch has that magic to bring out the potential in a manuscript. I am grateful to have had her brilliant insights enrich every sentence in this book. And a colossal thank-you and bravo to Lynn Douek, projects coordinator, for her exquisitely efficient production of this book.

A very special thank-you to all of the men and women who so

graciously allowed themselves to be interviewed and surveyed, as well as to my clients and students, whose lives and stories have touched me so profoundly.

I have no words to thank my closest friends Esther Solomon, Lisa Marcus, Ivy Kalazon, and Tova Lutz, my cousin Elana Dvir, and my dear sister Tova Harkavy for traveling yet another journey with me. Your love, encouragement, support, and feedback throughout this journey (and every other journey) are profoundly appreciated.

To my husband Aryeh: thank you for being so wonderfully different from me! And thank you for showing me what true loyalty and acceptance are really about. I am beyond fortunate to travel through life with you by my side. And to our children: it is fascinating to see how our efforts to appreciate our personality differences enabled us to appreciate – in each of you – your unique blend of personality traits. I hope I've enriched you as much as much as you've enriched me.

The stories and interviews in this book are about real people and their lives. However, all names and some details have been changed to protect the identities of the individuals involved.

Before You Read This Book

Personality differences! They never cease to amaze me. Most of us look for similarities when we choose a spouse. Yet, once married, we discover just how different we are. It seems that the old adage "opposites attract" is far from outdated. Over the years, I wondered what this attraction of opposites was all about; what was underlying and fueling this pull to someone so different from ourselves? One thing was clear: while some couples were stuck in a perpetual state of frustration and annoyance over their personality differences, others made their dissimilarities work for them and built happy, successful marriages. My intrigue grew; I wanted to know whether the successful couples shared a secret.

My search for an answer and my passion to help couples led to years of study and clinical work, and eventually to a research project. I surveyed hundreds of married people in the United States and personally interviewed a broad range of married and divorced people in eight different countries. (For an explanation of my research methodology, please turn to appendix A.)

The results were both fascinating and inspiring. Across the

globe, despite differences in culture, language, and religion, couples in good marriages used similar tools for making their personality differences work. These couples didn't have happy marriages *in spite* of their differences, but *because* of them. In other words, they didn't just *live* with their personality differences; they learned to *love* with their personality differences. I am very excited to share my findings with you in the following pages.

Although this book is filled with information and exercises to access the strength inherent in personality differences, the information can also be applied to gender differences, cultural differences, and many other types of differences.

TWO IMPORTANT SUGGESTIONS FOR READING THIS BOOK: In order for you to get the most out of this book – and ultimately, the most out of your marriage – **I highly recommend reading the following pages on your own**, without your spouse. The key to accessing the power within this book is to stay focused on yourself and *your* growth. Therefore, going solo on this read is the best thing for you and your duo.

Please also keep in mind that every marriage is unique. **It is essential not to compare your marriage to anyone else's**. No two marriages have the same texture or potential beauty. And often, it is impossible to see the true profoundness and beauty of a marriage from the outside.

My sincere hope is that the following pages will help you reveal and access the unique beauty in your own marriage.

"The only place you will find a perfectly matched pair is in the shoe store."

Dance with Your Differences

Chapter 1

The Light Switch

S he was attracted to him because he was *stable and practical*; once married, she got turned off because he was *drab and business-like*.

He was attracted to her because she *was fun and spontaneous*; once married, he got annoyed because she was *boisterous and unpredictable*.

She was attracted to him because he was *happy and funny*; once married, she got turned off because he was *naive and silly*.

He was attracted to her because *she reminded him of his mother*; once married, he got annoyed because she *reminded him of his mother*.

People say it all the time: "The *very things* that first attract you to your spouse often end up being the *very things* that annoy you." And these "very things" can even tear couples apart. Many spouses (of all ages) shrug their shoulders and passively give in to this "truth," slowly watching their marriages wilt. It's heartbreaking to see this pattern repeat itself over and over again. This heartbreak is what drove me to research this topic extensively and write this book – because I know the other side of this truth: those very things that attract us to our spouses have the power to invigorate our relationships. They have the power to give meaning and vitality to our marriages. If we use them correctly, they have the power to re-attract us to our spouses, over and over again.

For the majority of couples, those attracting/repelling factors are personality differences. The introvert who marries the extrovert. The spender who marries the saver. The organized person who marries the not-so-organized.

Personality differences have the potential to make your marriage… or break your marriage. This book will show you how to *make* your marriage. Together, in the following pages, we will learn how to shift perspective so that you can build the relationship you desire.

"Personality differences have the potential to make your marriage… or break your marriage. This book will show you how to *make* your marriage."

Why are personality differences so attractive (often subconsciously) in the beginning of a courtship? Because they promise something. And it's something that we all want: *completion*. Underlying the attraction to someone who is different from us is a sense of feeling complete with this other person.

Many people take issue with the idea that we need someone to "complete us." I agree with them! We shouldn't need someone to help us stand firmly on our own feet or feel good about ourselves. Completion is not dependency. So what do I mean by "completion"?

Take Lenny, one of the people in my relationship study, who

told me about his earliest encounters with his wife. "I felt really centered around Carla. It felt great. Her serious, quiet side brought out a part of me that I always wanted to have. And she loved my crazy, outgoing personality. I loved to watch her come out of herself around me." Lenny got a glimpse into who he could really become – centered and grounded – and what his relationship with Carla could become. In other words, he realized (partially subconsciously) that their completion as a couple would also be a doorway – and shortcut – to his own individual completion.

A few months after the wedding, however, Lenny started getting frustrated with Carla's reserved nature. "Now that we're married, it's so frustrating. She is so serious, and when we go out, she is really quiet. Why can't she just interact with people?" We can all relate to Lenny's annoyance. The energy flowed so easily in the beginning. Now it just did not.

But the story is as follows: the completion we initially feel with our spouses is like a free gift – to show us the potential of what we can have. Then, the training wheels are taken off; this is when every couple needs to put some efforts in, to make that completion real.

If we want to succeed in *anything*, we need to make some effort. If we want to be great athletes, we need to work out. If we want to be great doctors, we need to invest years of study. And if we want to attain the completion we experienced while we were dating, both on a personal level and on a relationship level, we need to put in effort.

We all have an independent part of ourselves that might struggle with this idea. On some level, we want to believe that we can become completed individuals on our own. Why should we need to get married to do this? Here's an analogy: marriage is like a jam session. If you want to make great music with someone else, what's the prerequisite? To play solo. But if you can play solo, this doesn't mean that you can automatically jam. Only when you play with others do you realize where you're out of tune and/or out of rhythm.

In life, no matter how well we play solo, we will never see ourselves as we truly are – and therefore can never come into our true potential – until we can successfully jam with someone else. We spend a lot of time playing solo, but *only* when we get super close with someone – specifically in the lifelong, committed relationship of marriage – will we *see and understand* where we need fine tuning in order to grow into the happiest, most loving versions of ourselves. Although other types of relationships assist us in this, only marriage – that lifelong commitment to one's partner – has the power to show us who we truly are … and truly can become. AND help us to get there!

Completion in Marriage

There are two types of completion in marriage: personal balance and teamwork/synergy.

Completion Type 1: Personal Balance

We can become more balanced, developed people through marriage, specifically due to our spouses' opposite personality traits.

Ancient Judaic sources explain that a couple's personality differences go way beyond being OK: they are the major benefit of the marriage. A renowned Jewish sage, the Chatam Sofer, clarifies that personality differences are the key to a balanced marriage because our personality differences encourage (and sometimes nudge) us to become more balanced individuals.* For example,

---

* Rabbi Moshe Sofer, a leading Judaic seminal thinker, in his nineteenth-century work *Torat Moshe* (Jerusalem: Chatam Sofer Institute, 1972) on Genesis 24:50.

Lenny wanted to become more centered and grounded, and he ultimately succeeded in this because Carla's seriousness brought out this potential in him. It definitely takes some effort to achieve personal balance, but the rewards far exceed the effort.

We all wish that marriage were easy. Although it's not easy, when we have the right attitude and make the right efforts, we create an ease in the relationship. The more we make these efforts, the more ease and joy we create. The completion mindset has the power to ease up your marriage in a huge way, because when you think completion, you actually flip on a light in your marriage. I'm not exaggerating when I say that a couple can be sitting in darkness and discontent, and within seconds, the light is shining bright. I've seen it happen, countless times. It's a choice – just like everything else in life – and when we make this choice, we empower ourselves and our marriages. The dividends are huge.

Here's an example of personal balance in action:

BRIAN: When I first meet people, I am shy. But since being with my wife Suzanne – who is a lot more outgoing and social than I am – I'm definitely not as shy as I used to be, and I'm able to break the ice a lot quicker than before.

CHANA: How did that happen? Did she try to change you?

BRIAN: To be honest, I think I changed myself. Suzanne goes out of her way to speak to strangers. I don't. But because I am with her when she engages with strangers, I obviously can't just stand there and be rude. In the beginning, I had to push myself to get involved in the conversation, which was really annoying at first. But I did push myself and tried to adapt, and before you know it, I'm as bad as she is ... or as good as she is. So I guess I stretched enough times and although it was hard, I'm so glad I did it.

CHANA: On a scale from zero to ten, with zero being totally

introverted and ten being totally extroverted, where would you put your wife?

BRIAN: I'd say a ten. But since she's not extroverted in an in-your-face way, I'd give her a seven. She's super warm and friendly. I'm somewhere in the middle, a five or six. But you know, before I met her, I was quite reserved, probably a two or three.

By spending time with his wife, Brian went from a two or three all the way to a five or six.

This is what Suzanne has to say about the changes in their marriage:

SUZANNE: The big difference in our marriage is that I'm a lot louder and probably a bit more opinionated. Brian is a lot more placid and calm. He's more of an introvert. When we met, I was immediately attracted to his calm, gentle nature.

CHANA: On a scale from zero to ten, with zero being total introvert and ten total extrovert, where are you, and where is your husband?

SUZANNE: I would probably say that I'm a seven or eight and he's a four. This difference between us is quite obvious. People who meet us know that he's the one that keeps me a little bit more grounded. And I think my outgoingness pulls him out of his shell a little bit more. I think he used to get walked all over a lot more than he does now, just from being that kind, gentle, anything-to-have-an-easy-life kind of person.

We've really rubbed off on each other. It's nice, though; we've evolved into the happy medium. I wouldn't say it was a natural process; there were a lot of bumps on the road. We both stretched. But you know, if it weren't for having someone like him, I would probably just jet off around the world and do random things the whole time. I would never really settle, but he keeps me grounded.

In just a few years of marriage, Suzanne and Brian already balanced each other out tremendously. You'd think that introverts would marry introverts and extroverts would marry extroverts. Or grounded people would marry grounded people and spontaneous dreamers would marry dreamers. But typically, this is not the case, because the grounded people need the spontaneous dreamers to get their imaginations in motion. And the spontaneous dreamers need the grounded people to keep them from getting lost in the clouds. *It's all about balance.*

The reason the concept of completion is so powerful is that it allows us to see the deep, inner wisdom hidden within the spousal match – that is, the reason we're so well suited for each other. When our personality differences surface, all of a sudden our relationships make less sense. Typically, this is when people start to question their marriages. But *this* is where the power of completion comes in: when we see how we can balance each other out, the light flips on. Things really start to make sense, and we understand why our spouses are *our* spouses.

As I celebrate my twenty-seventh year of marriage, I am blown away by the many levels of completion I see within my own marriage (not to mention the completion I have been privy to, in hundreds of other people's marriages). As we mature and our marriages mature, we are able to see the wisdom of our matches more and more clearly. It is my deepest hope that as you read the pages of this book and apply the exercises, you will reveal, with every passing year, this wisdom in your own life.

Personal Balance in a Nutshell

We can become more balanced, developed people through marriage, specifically because of our spouses' different personality traits:

- When we spend time together, each spouse's personality differences naturally rub off on each other (without a lot of effort).

- Our spouses' differences in personality nudge us to grow because our shortcomings are highlighted (this takes effort).

- Our spouses serve as role models for a particular behavior; as a result, that behavior becomes more accessible to us.

Completion Type 2: Teamwork/Synergy

Let's take a look at the second type of completion in marriage.

Because of our complementary differences, our team potential is exponentially greater than our solo potential.

If you want to open up a business, you start small. Typically, you don't have the resources or capital to do otherwise. You work hard to develop your one-man business. But when you want to go big, if you want to be a thriving enterprise, you usually have to collaborate with others. If you're smart, you look for people who have skills and abilities that you don't have.

So too in marriage. If you want to go far in life, partner with someone who shares your vision and whose skills and abilities will complement yours. *Marriage is the ultimate team, the ultimate synergy.* If you complement and complete each other in this way, you can become much more than the sum of your parts. This truth is best expressed by an African proverb: "If you want to go fast, go alone ... if you want to go far, go together."

Here is an example of teamwork/synergy in action:

LANCE: My wife is the antithesis of me and my family...my parents, siblings...all of us. We are all loud, there's always yelling, everyone is nervous. At six a.m., my mother is already pounding chicken cutlets, everything is already wild. Lori comes from the extreme opposite – a family of calm and quiet. It hypnotized me! I wanted it to be part of my life. All of our differences are connected to the fact that I'm a doer and my wife is a "be-er." I'm the nervous type who wants things to be done immediately...to an unhealthy extreme. If it's possible to push something off until later, Lori has no problem doing so. There are also cultural differences: she's from a warm southern background and I'm from a cold city background. Hugs, warmth, intimacy...these are things that I didn't grow up with in my family.

LORI: I would agree with Lance's description. He is always going from one thing to the next, trying to attain something. I'm more quiet and satisfied. I'm happy where I am, not in a hurry. It can be very frustrating sometimes. For example, in the evening, he has a whole list of things to do for tomorrow morning, and sometimes we never have that time to sit and talk. But there's the upside, big time. There are many things that are hard for me to do because I'm too laid-back and don't like confrontation.

LANCE: So true! There is a strength and a sharpness that comes from my side of the family. Sometimes Lori says, "Wow, I would never be able to say that to the children's teacher." She's grateful that I know how to stick up for our kids. On the other hand, growing up, my mother never said "I love you" – expressions of intimacy made her nervous. But because of the warm, loving way Lori talks to me and our kids, our daughters express their feelings openly and without holding back. They say "I love you" all the time, even to my mother. These words just roll off their tongues with kisses and hugs. This has even helped my mother grow. Today, she's able to say to the grandchildren, "I love you." Our marriage is a good mix of softness and strength.

Because Lance and Lori's differences complement each other, they have become much more than the sum of their parts. Each "player" in their marriage has proficiencies that the other lacks. This is what allows their "team" to be so successful. As Lance expressed, "There's a strength and sharpness that comes from my side of the family." Because of this "gift," Lori has the benefit of a husband who can stick up for their kids. Because each of the partners has different strengths, their children (and even their extended family!) are enriched.

A Note to Singles

When I speak about personality differences, I am often asked the following question: "Are you suggesting that when dating, people should look for someone who is different from themselves? Is that the goal?" The answer is a definitive no! As I explain, I am not suggesting that if, for example, you're an extrovert, you must marry an introvert. Don't worry: *if you're attracted, the differences will be there*! Sooner or later they'll show up. (Keep in mind, however, that similarity in values and ideals is very important to look for.) You see, even if two extroverts get married, they will tend to be extroverted in different ways. And if not, they will end up having other personality differences between them.

What about Similarities?

We all know that a lasting, vibrant marriage needs both comfort/ safety and excitement/renewal. Therefore, both similarities and differences play important roles in a marriage. Similarities, on a rational, *conscious* level, play a big role in the decision to marry a particular person. And although similarities are a source of safety in a relationship, safe can become boring and monotonous. Our differences – challenge and all – can be a source of excitement, expansion, and renewed attraction, when we know how to dance with them. It's specifically when we learn how to work the "tension of opposites" that we can access the well of chemistry and vitality hidden within our personality differences.

This book is dedicated to showing you how to dance with your differences; chapter 4 will explore the role of similarities in this dance.

What about Extreme Differences?

Before going further, I want to clarify that although differences can be a tremendous asset, this does not mean that the extreme introvert is a good match for an extreme extrovert. Or that the extreme spender is a match for the extreme saver. Radical, polarized differences might create challenges that are very difficult to bridge. On a scale from zero to ten, with ten being an extreme extrovert and zero being an extreme introvert, a zero and a ten will be an extremely challenging marriage (although I *have* seen people make extreme differences work in a marriage when they put in the extra time and effort). However, a four and a nine or a three and an eight could work well together, if they work on completing and balancing each other out.

On a flight, a guy told me about his extremely organized

personality; not surprisingly, he came from a family that is super clean and organized. He went out with a woman, and when he got a glimpse of her apartment, he almost fainted. He said, "It looked like a tornado hit it. I mean, even her cleaning supplies were dirty and dusty. And then, as I'm taking in the scene, she says to me, 'I'm so glad that I had a chance to clean my apartment before you came over.' I think I was in shock." Wisely, this was their last date.

Note: If you have this kind of extreme, polarized difference in your marriage, do not freak out! Yes, it will take more effort to work things out, but I've seen many couples pull it off. Keep reading; the tools in this book will prove very helpful.

The only time that I encourage people to look for a future spouse who is very different in personality is when they have a negative character trait that they really struggle with. For example, if someone struggles in a big way with anger or anxiety, it would be wise to look for a more patient or calm spouse. However, keep in mind what I mentioned earlier: it is not wise to look for the radical opposite of oneself.

When two people meet, the completion is all there, in potential. Marriage is the awesome journey of actualizing this potential. When people who feel stuck in their marriages internalize this truth, they feel liberated. They realize that we all have a tremendous amount of power to determine the success of our marriages.

The Rude Awakening

When Erin met her husband, she felt a magnetic attraction toward him. Charlie had a beaming smile and a cheerful, easygoing approach to life – nothing phased him. After the wedding, however, Erin saw the flip side of this character trait.

"For me, it was a 'rude awakening,'" Erin told me.

ERIN: A rude woman cut him in line once and he said, "She's probably rushing because of some emergency." I couldn't believe my ears. I would never call myself a pessimist; rather, I am a proud realist. My feet are always on the ground and I can clearly see things for what they are. OK, maybe sometimes I'm too quick to judge, but no one's perfect. Charlie, on the other hand, is an optimist – the cheerful, "cup is half full" type. He always sees the good in people, even when there's very little good to see. He often gets taken advantage because of this, both in business deals and personal relationships. Lately, he's been trying to convince me that my narcissistic, obnoxious, controlling boss actually cares about his employees. Could I really have married someone so naive?

Like many couples, Erin and Charlie were initially attracted by each other's opposite qualities. Here's Charlie's side of the story:

CHARLIE: I've always thought of myself as a happy, satisfied guy. Sure, I have my share of frustrations and disappointments – but overall, I'm a positive man. Erin is more judgmental than I am; she's quick to be on the defense. I realize that she's bright and can read into what people say and how they behave. But her first impressions are not always accurate, which is really frustrating for me. And she doesn't recognize that people can change. Take, for example, a few months ago, when we were trying to negotiate a deal with a used car salesman. From the get-go, she decided that he wasn't trustworthy at all. As we were nearing the close of the deal, we got stuck on some details. That's when Erin got fed up and said, "He's trying to rip us off. Let's leave!" OK, maybe I'm too quick to trust people, but if she weren't so negative, I think that we could've worked out a good deal.

The Challenge of the Gift

As we clarified above, the very thing that attracts us often becomes the very thing that annoys us. Sure enough, when I asked Erin what most attracted her to Charlie, she cited his "positive energy and outlook." Likewise, Charlie told me that he loved Erin's "realistic, pragmatic, down-to-earth personality." So why was there so much frustration after they got married?

Let's first try to understand *how* this annoyance festers and surfaces.

Erin and Charlie's mutual attraction was definitely fueled by their personality differences; they felt that sense of completion we discussed earlier. Each of them was able to clearly express the positive traits that the other was bringing to the relationship (which was a result of their differences). What they didn't realize, however, is that while every positive character trait that we bring into our marriages is a gift, these gifts come with a price tag – a challenge. For example:

Gift	Challenge
Givers	Tend to struggle with setting and keeping boundaries
Organizers	Typically struggle with rigidity and some intolerance
Laid-back folks	Commonly struggle with disorganization or laziness or carelessness
Analytical folks	Tend to struggle with being critical and/or pessimistic
Ambitious people	Typically struggle with prioritization of relationships and leisure activities

Erin's "realistic, pragmatic" side came with its challenge: judgment and negativity. Charlie's "positive, cheerful" side came with its challenge: naiveté.

When we date, we are usually so enraptured by the gifts our future spouses bring that we don't notice the challenges that accompany these presents. Then we get married, and annoyance flares because on a subconscious (and sometimes even conscious level), we want the gifts – without the price. The fantasy of getting only the gift can threaten to kill our hope of *ever* having good marriages. People are a package deal.

Here's what I've seen, over and over again, in my practice and research: *problems in a marriage often set in when we forget the gift and focus on the challenge*; this is when completion goes out the window.

That's what happened with Erin and Charlie. The more they focused on their "annoying differences," the wider the gap between them grew. Charlie became the family spokesman for positivity… and tried desperately to bring Erin around to his way of thinking. Erin began to lecture regularly about the danger of naiveté and tried to pull Charlie into a more rational perspective on life. Instead of completing each other, they were battling each other. Erin and Charlie were trapped – not in a bad marriage but rather in a tug of war.

It's funny, in my many years working as a dating coach, no one has ever said to me, "I'm looking for an uptight, rigid partner!" But if someone is looking for an efficient, organized person, some uptightness tends to come with the territory.

Likewise, when people feel an attraction to a laid-back person, they are not thinking, "Wow, I really hope this person is disorganized or spacey." But the messiness (or a similar challenge) tends to come with the territory. Again, it's a package deal.

Spiraling Down – And Up

OK, so now we can admit it: we are all putting up with our spouses' challenges. So how is anyone supposed to be happily married?

People who are thriving in their marriages remember a very important thing: our spouses are also dealing with *our* challenges (that accompany our gifts).

We fall into a negative cycle when we:

- Forget that our initial attraction was just an inkling of the completion we can potentially have with our partners (see earlier in this chapter)
- Focus on our spouses' challenges instead of their gifts
- Forget that our spouses are also dealing with our challenges

I call this negative cycle a downward spiral, It's totally human to start heading down this spiral. As a matter of fact, if we aren't conscious of it, this often happens naturally.

But we can choose a better response, just as Charlie and Erin did. The work we did together enabled them to choose to:

- See their personality differences through the eyes of completion
- Remember that their spouses were putting up with their challenges
- Focus on the gifts each was bringing into the marriage

This is when they were able to turn their marriage around. In fact, today they are thriving. Chapters 3–9 will explore how to do this. We will learn how to ascend an upward spiral toward a respectful, loving marriage. With the right way of thinking, we can flip on the light in our marriages. We can *choose* whether we experience light or darkness from our personality differences.

The Power of One

As you're reading this, you might be thinking, "Well, if my spouse would read this book, we'd be in great shape. How's it going to help if I'm the only one reading it? We're supposed to be a team."

Actually, it only takes *one* person to flip the light on in a marriage. You can take your relationship to the next level even if your spouse is not on board. That's because a marriage is a system; if one side changes, it will automatically create a change in the relationship dynamic. Although it's impossible to change your spouse, it *is* possible to become the reason he or she changes (even if your spouse is not conscious of your efforts). Fact is, even if your spouse never changes, there will still be more light in your marriage, from the brightness created through your work alone.

"A marriage is a system; if one side changes, it will automatically create a change in the relationship dynamic."

Before we get to the upward spiral, let's understand the downward spiral better; we need to know what to avoid.

Chapter 2

The Downward Spiral

They say that no man is an island. I disagree. No matter how socially connected we are, we still have our own ways of thinking, feeling, and behaving. Each one of us really *is* an island. But although we might really enjoy our independent existence, it can be quite lonely. The question marriage asks is: How successfully can we bridge the distance to someone else's island?

Our spouses have their own islands, on which there are *different* ways of thinking, feeling, and behaving. The natural, knee-jerk reaction to these differences is judgment. Since I am right, my spouse must be wrong, weird, abnormal, etc.

We feel good on our own islands. Our spouses' islands are unfamiliar – and even threatening at times – because they stretch us out of our comfort zones. Why do people say that life begins at the end of your comfort zone? Because a comfort zone becomes boring, dull, and limiting; all of the really good stuff happens when we stretch beyond ourselves.

The good news is that marriage is the shortcut to going beyond the limitations of a comfort zone. The first step is to adjust our expectations.

Everyone goes into marriage with expectations. On a subconscious level, almost everyone walking down the aisle thinks, "My spouse is just like me and will join me on *my* path so that I will no longer be alone."

Then reality hits and the rude awakening comes: "I can't believe we're so different! Why didn't I see this before?"

If we do not apply the wisdom we learned in chapter 1 – that our differences hold the power of completion and our gifts come with challenges – we might find ourselves falling into a downward spiral. This is what it looks like:

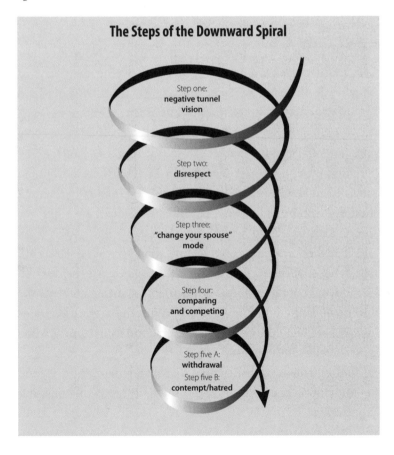

The Steps of the Downward Spiral

Step one:
negative tunnel vision

Step two:
disrespect

Step three:
"change your spouse" mode

Step four:
comparing and competing

Step five A:
withdrawal

Step five B:
contempt/hatred

STEP ONE: NEGATIVE TUNNEL VISION

We ignore our partners' gifts and focus on the challenges. We put a negative spin on our personality differences, equating different with bad.

STEP TWO: DISRESPECT

Being judgmental about our differences leads to a lack of respect.

STEP THREE: "CHANGE YOUR SPOUSE" MODE

In order to "improve" the relationship, we set out to change our spouses to be more like us.

STEP FOUR: COMPARING AND COMPETING

Our negative views of our spouses are magnified when we hold them up to those around us.

The next step is one or both of the following:

STEP FIVE A: WITHDRAWAL

As our negativity increases, our attraction fades and we start to live separate lives.

STEP FIVE B: CONTEMPT/HATRED

Negativity blooms into outright loathing.

NOTE: obviously, this spiral is not set in stone; steps might be skipped and/or in a different order for some people.

Let's explore some real-life examples to see what the five-step downward spiral looks like in action.

Step One: Negative Focus on Differences

Bill and Fran were in pretty bad shape when I met them. Bill wanted a divorce; Fran was begging him to stay and try harder. He was so fed up with Fran that he could hardly look at her. His body language screamed "I can't stand you."

As I listened to their story, it became clear what was going on. Bill was annoyed with Fran's tendency to be too serious. True to my experience with couples, the point of greatest conflict was the original point of greatest attraction. The thing that had most attracted Bill to Fran in the beginning was her seriousness; his first wife couldn't hold a deep discussion for more than three minutes.

When Bill dated Fran, he reveled in their serious conversations. But once married, he started to get annoyed; it seemed to him that Fran turned every conversation into a heavy interaction.

In an almost predictable pattern, our reactions to personality differences change at certain points in our relationships:

- PRE-MARRIAGE. In this infatuated stage of the relationship, we tend to gloss over personality differences; they might even be seen as endearing.
- EARLY MARRIAGE. We tell ourselves that the differences will fade and disappear over time, or pale in comparison to the similarities.
- ESTABLISHED MARRIAGE. After the dust settles, the differences start to annoy us. Furthermore, the similarities begin to pale in comparison (if we can see them at all).

Take the classic case of an introvert marrying an extrovert. While they are dating, the introvert feels so much freer and able to interact socially (because of the energy of the extrovert). The extrovert feels more grounded (because of the energy of the introvert). They get married, and then the trouble begins. The extrovert wants to go out and have fun; the introvert wants to stay home. The extrovert wants to invite company over; the introvert feels drained by the thought. Usually, they will try to change each other, which only leads to more pain, frustration, and anger.

At this point in the process, if we . . .

- interpret our personality differences as negative;
- forget the inherent gifts and completion held within the differences;
- concentrate on what we *don't* have in common and stop seeing all that we *do* have in common (the importance of similarities will be discussed in chapter 4);

…the gap between our personality differences grows even wider.

Step Two: Annoyance and Disrespect

Eventually, Bill decided that Fran was just a heavy, cumbersome person, and before he knew it, he was annoyed by her whole being. He couldn't stand being around her. He put all his efforts into trying to change her into a lighter person.

Bill went through all three of the distinct levels of annoyance, which usually build on each other:

1. SPECIFIC ANNOYANCE. Upset with the specific actions of your spouse: "Why did my spouse walk off while we had guests in the house to go and do something alone?"

2. GENERAL ANNOYANCE. Upset with the underlying attitude of your spouse: "My spouse's whole attitude toward people is annoying!"

3. GLOBAL ANNOYANCE. Upset with your spouse's presence: "My spouse's whole being annoys me!"

At this point, many of us go into blame mode: "It's my spouse's fault for not being the type of person I want. Really, I'm the good guy, putting up with my spouse!" These negative thoughts, when unchecked, breed disrespect.

Disrespect is so easily communicated, in ways we often don't realize. Even subtle expressions of disrespect are destructive, such as:

- Not paying attention to your spouse (a form of ignoring)
- Making light of a concern your partner considers important
- Mocking or dismissing your spouse through body language

I worked with Fran and Bill for a few months and watched their marriage turn around. How did this happen? Bill explained:

BILL: I started to remember our dating days and realized that I was totally taking our deep conversations for granted. As my eyes opened, I also began to realize that Fran was also putting up with my "stuff" – I know that I have an annoying tendency to micromanage everyone around me. My ex-wife used to throw this in my face all the time ... she called me "controlling."

When Bill realized that in contrast to his ex-wife, Fran was successful in keeping her annoyance at bay, he felt challenged to do the same and return the favor. By refocusing his *thoughts*, Bill changed how he *felt* about Fran, which led to the turnaround in their marriage.

Annoyance is tricky; at first, it seems like a petty, trivial emotion. But when it's not controlled (or harnessed for the good), it can quickly push a good marriage into further descent.

Step Three: "Change Your Spouse" Mode

Anthony's wife was fixated on changing him, as he explained in our interview:

ANTHONY: My wife is so exacting and demanding – even when she cooks, she puts so much into it that it takes all of her energy. Problem is, she then expects me to do the same. When we go out, she wants me to guess what she wants. I'll plan a date, but her expectations are so high, I feel like whatever I do won't be enough. I lose all of my ability to think of any good ideas because there's so much pressure.

The crazy thing is that guys at work always ask me what to do in order to be romantic, but right now I'm stuck in my own marriage. It bothers me because I'm so spontaneous in everything I do, but here I'm stuck. She needs something from me, something romantic...but my romantic side is blocked because of the pressure.

Anthony brilliantly articulated what happens to us when we feel someone is trying to change us. On the best of days, this kind of constant pressure can cause us to at least partially shut down. On the worst days, we get angry, hurt, and might rebel or withdraw. Ironically, when Anthony's wife turned him into a project, instead of getting more from him, she ended up getting less – partially because she was distancing him from his vitality by trying to change him.

It's almost inevitable: once disrespect seeps in, you'll try to change your spouse. This behavior stems from the erroneous belief that "*if only* you were more like me, I'd love you more." This is the same mistake Bill made with Fran: he put all his efforts into making her into a "lighter" person because he was convinced that this would improve their relationship. Most of us fall into this "if only" type of thinking: if only my spouse were more social, tuned in, kind, tough, proper, relaxed, and so on...You'll notice that this way of thinking is entirely other-focused; when we get trapped in this mindset, we conveniently forget our own shortcomings.

Also, when we fall into "change your spouse" mode, we lose some of our compassion. We think, "Why can't my spouse just get it, already?" We forget that even though we may be very developed in a certain trait (such as being socially graceful), our spouses may need to try ten times harder to exhibit even a fraction of our social graces. Certainly, we cannot make them change. *The only person you can change is yourself.*

There is a cute joke about a Buddhist hotdog vendor in

Manhattan who sold hotdogs for $2 a piece. A man handed him a $20 bill and waited for his change back. After a few minutes, the vendor still wasn't looking for change, so the customer said, "Hey, buddy, where's my change?" The Buddhist vendor replied: "Change comes from within." A good laugh, but it's true: real, lasting change does have to come from within.

In marriage, every spouse has a constant choice: to get into the driver's seat and travel forward, or to slide into neutral. If you slide into neutral, the downward spiral just happens.

"Every spouse has a constant choice: to get into the driver's seat and travel forward, or to slide into neutral. If you slide into neutral, the downward spiral just happens."

Step Four: Comparing and Competing

Claire opened up to me: "I'm really frustrated. My husband Jerry and I have been spending time with a few other couples. I watch these other husbands debating and expressing smart ideas, and Jerry just sits there. You know, it's really embarrassing." I gave Claire an understanding smile, remembering her single days, when I worked with her as a dating coach. She used to tell me over and over again, "I need to marry a warm, sensitive, honest, and loyal guy. It's not a tall order, is it? I've dated the smart, impressive types – I know I could never marry one of them." I gently reminded Claire that she got her warm, sensitive, honest, and loyal guy. She laughed. "Wow…weird…it's so easy for me to forget this."

Why did Claire do this? Why do *we* do this? One reason is that we want it all. Let's face it: today's consumer mentality has gotten into our psyche. Since everything is disposable and replaceable, we start asking ourselves, "Is there maybe someone better out there, who could fill *all* of my needs?" And the consumer-centric voice within us says, "Is my spouse making *me* happy? Maybe he/she got the better deal? Is my husband/wife devaluing the net worth of *my* commodity (my marriage)?" We feel a sense of entitlement to get everything we want.

What drives consumerism is the endless promise of "more and better"; what drives love is loyalty, trust, and commitment. "More and better" is a bottomless pit that can potentially cheat us out of *ever* having a stable marriage.

How can Claire get back on track in her marriage? By consciously spending time focusing on Jerry's positive, unique qualities – and why she married him in the first place.

Here's how the comparing process works:

- When we forget our spouses' positive, unique qualities, we compare them to other men and women.
- When we forget our own personal positive, unique qualities, we compare ourselves to other people.
- When we forget the unique positive qualities of our marriages, we compare our marriages to other people's marriages.

One of my favorite parts of being a marriage counselor is the bird's-eye view I have of each couple's unique match. I love this, because I can see that every marriage has a "personality," a unique tapestry. When we don't appreciate the unique specialness of our marriages, we start comparing them with other people's marriages, which in turn sucks the life out of our own. Theodore Roosevelt said it well: "Comparison is the thief of joy."

Appreciate the Uniqueness

When we waste our time comparing our marriages to other people's, we are unable to see and appreciate the unique strength of our own unions. Asking yourself these questions will help you get in touch with the strength of your marriage:

- What is one thing that is unique in yourself?
- What is one thing that is unique in your spouse?
- What is one thing that is unique in your marriage, at the best of times?
- What is one thing that is unique in your marriage – particularly in the way your personality differences balance each other out?

The next step on the downward spiral could either be the withdrawal of step five A or the anger of step five B.

Step Five A: Withdrawal and Living Separate Lives

Were you ever shocked to hear that a marriage you considered strong, sturdy, and good is breaking up? True, we never know what goes on behind closed doors. But strangely enough, many couples do not fight and argue their way into a divorce. The opposite – many divorcing couples seem to be living a tranquil existence. But underneath this apparent tranquility is often relationship boredom, apathy, emotional withdrawal, and/or coldness.

This is especially true for midlife divorces. Former vice president Al Gore and his wife Tipper joined many older couples in citing "growing apart" as the reason they split. Many older couples describe their marriages as "stale." Sometimes, one or both partners are fully immersed in work, hobbies, or other interests. When the partners no longer make the effort to share that major part of their lives with each other, what's left? It's usually just shared chores, which may include childcare – not exactly an interesting and attractive relationship. Although some couples can maintain their marriage on this level, others go on to divorce. At this point in the downward spiral, some sort of intervention by a third party is often necessary, e.g., marriage counselor, coach, clergy, etc.

Warning Signs of Parallel or Separate Lives

The following signs may indicate your relationship is heading toward parallel and/or separate lives.

- You exchange information through notes, texts, e-mail, notes on the fridge... or as you pass by each other, rather than engaging in direct communication.
- You forget to ask about each other's important presentations, meetings, exams, etc.
- Your give all your attention to your work, children, or house-related technical issues.
- You ignore or forget significant milestones in your marriage, such as anniversaries.
- You no longer discuss the day's activities together.
- When you do interact, it's practical. You talk about the bills, the chores, and the kids. Discussions about meaningful things with positive emotional content are avoided.
- You socialize separately.
- There is very little or no physical affection or intimacy.
- You no longer feel like allies, on the same team.

Step Five B: Contempt and Hatred

When Melanie and Tom stepped into my office, I immediately felt the cold emotional distance between them. They sat at opposite ends of the couch and refused to look at each other. Actually, they hadn't really talked in several months. When I asked them what first attracted them to each other, they could hardly remember, even though they had only been married four years. They made it clear that their visit to me was their last-ditch effort; they had already filed for divorce.

I told them that they were wasting their time if they thought that *I* could save their marriage; only they could. My question to them was, "Do you want this marriage to work out?" They both admitted some degree of desire for it to work; they had a child together, both were on second marriages, and they did not look forward to yet another divorce.

At one point, they actually started to engage in a positive conversation . . . a glimmer of hope. But then Tom said, "You're always busy helping everyone out. So what if this neighbor had a C-section in her eighth month! You took care of her enough! You don't know when to stop!" Melanie retorted, "I never help her out on your time. What do you care? It's not costing you a cent! You're so selfish, you're so negative – you only think about yourself!" Tom snapped, "We are too different! Every day, I realize it more and more. You're all over the place, trying to please the whole world. It's only because you hate yourself. I only think about myself? You have no boundaries. You only give because you're insecure. Ugh . . . how did I marry someone like you?"

Hatred is contagious. When one partner starts to release the hatred vibe, it's really hard for the other partner to resist sending it right back. Being judgmental is a portal to hatred. Before you know it, the couple is playing hatred ping-pong. From here, it only gets uglier. Once again, it's those very personality differences that potentially promise growth and completion that end up becoming big thorns in a relationship when viewed through a critical lens.

Caution: it is very important to differentiate between making the statement "I hate you," which a spouse might yell in a moment of rage, and actually being in a state of hatred. Just because someone says "I hate you" (which should be avoided at all cost) doesn't mean it's true. Often, it isn't.

When a couple is truly stuck in hatred mode, I work with them separately. The most important question I independently ask each partner is, "Even if this marriage did not work out, what do you need to work on in yourself, in order to be a better person and spouse? Because even if you get divorced and want to remarry, chances are that you will bring your 'stuff' into your next marriage, unless you work it out beforehand. The profound truth is, wherever you go . . . there you are. You can't run away from yourself."

Tom and Melanie were able to take a sober look at themselves and admit their respective "stuff."

This is the only way to successfully step out of blame mode, which many couples fall into. It's just so much easier to see what our spouses are doing wrong. Melanie admitted that she has needed to work on her boundaries since childhood. This was something she had always wanted to fix. Likewise, Tom realized that his judgmental, critical nature was creating problems in every area of his life. He also owned up to his anger issues.

It took a lot of time, sweat, and tears, but they made it. The key was for both of them to own their own problems, step out of blame mode, and let go of the negative narrative they had composed about each other. As their hatred started to thaw, moments of civility began to seep into their relationship, and, eventually, glimpses of love began to shine through. The second part of this book, "The Upward Spiral," will outline the process I followed with Tom and Melanie – and so many others – to reverse the downward spiral and begin ascending an upward spiral toward a loving and rewarding marriage.

Although I try very hard to help couples avoid divorce (by helping them find the adhesive force between them), there are times when divorce is the only option. Specifically, if there is untreated mental illness, abuse, or unchecked addictions, divorce might be the only solution. This being said, although there are other situations and scenarios that seem hopeless, having seen some of the worst marriages turn around, I am a big believer in the marriage process.

The encouraging news about hatred is that it can flip around … if we work hard on our thought processes. Truth is, we can all manufacture hatred. All we have to do is intensely focus on something we don't like about a person. If we stay in that tunnel vision for a long time, tell ourselves a negative narrative about that person, forget the positives, and forget that we're also flawed, we can spiral right into hatred. But we can also do the reverse – we can use our thoughts to produce love.

Sometimes, we need to hit rock bottom in order to make serious changes in ourselves. But as J. K. Rowling once said, "Rock bottom became the solid foundation upon which I rebuilt my life." For anyone who hits steps five A and B, rock bottom in a marriage typically requires quality professional help. In addition, the next few chapters will guide you in rebuilding your marriage.

More information for the various steps along the downward spiral can be found in appendix B. Meanwhile, it's time for the exciting stuff: the upward spiral.

The Upward Spiral

Step One: Refocus

Step Two: Tap into Completion

Step Three: Accept and Allow

Chapter 3

Hands-On Tools for Positive Change

My first book, *I Only Want to Get Married Once,* is essentially a dating manual for choosing the right marriage partner. A main theme in the book is that infatuation can serve as a jump start to a happy marriage, but it cannot sustain a marriage. After all, infatuation – that effortless, fantasy-driven obsession with another person that you experience at the beginning of a romantic relationship – can only last two or three years max. That's why it's so important – during the dating process – to make sure that there's something else there besides the infatuation, as well as something that can nurture a lasting attraction to each other. What is this something else that serves as a solid foundation for a lasting, loving marriage? A combination of five things (outlined in my first book): shared values, trust, respect, healthy boundaries, and good communication.

Let's take the concept of infatuation one step further. Infatuation is an interesting thing. Each one of us is capable of being infatuated with many people. And if we're really good at it, we're capable of being infatuated with a few different people in one day. But we couldn't marry most of these people. Actually, most of them would be disastrous matches for us – e.g., the upper class girl who is obsessed with the guy in the band (who lives from hand to mouth). Or the guy who needs a quiet, domestic type of wife but is infatuated with the fly-by-night, life-of-the-party girl.

Hollywood is all about the infatuation stage of relationships – the romance, the rapture – followed by the *effortless* "happily ever after." OK, real life isn't quite like that. But every lie has an element of truth in it. The truth in the lie of "happily ever after" is that you can have happily ever *after…after* a lot of effort. You see, Hollywood is missing the best part of the love story, which happens post-infatuation. This is when a couple recognizes that much of their initial attraction stemmed from the innate sense of completion they felt with each other. When they make the effort to grow closer and closer, they create a beautiful private love story that becomes increasingly profound with passing years.

It has been said that when you get married, you're actually tying the knot with three people: the imaginary person you are infatuated with, the actual person you're marrying, and the developed person your spouse will become over the years, largely as a consequence of the growth afforded by your marriage. Marriage is a journey of becoming – becoming more than we think we can be. One of my favorite parts of the journey is finding out who we can become as a result of being married to our spouses – and who they can become, as a result of being married to us.

Our personality differences are vital aspects of this journey. Although personality similarities are very important (as we'll clarify in the next chapter), it's actually our differences that open the door to a fulfilling relationship. They cause us to grow and expand our minds. They revitalize and energize our marriages. As I've seen so many times, it's often those very "annoying" personality differences that hold the power for a fantastic marriage, if only we know how to navigate the differences as they arise.

"Although personality similarities are very important, it's actually our differences that open the door to a fulfilling relationship."

Unfortunately, many couples don't know how to do this. Instead of using their personality differences to propel their marriages forward, they become repelled by their differences, therefore causing the relationship to start to unravel.

Helene and Eric were stuck in this stage when I met them. This is how Helene described her side of the story:

HELENE: It's almost like my husband Eric is two different people. When we're alone, he gives me undivided attention – whether I'm talking about big ideas or everyday stuff. I bask in the full attention I get. But as soon as other people are around, I feel almost insignificant. It's like I become his associate – there by his side while he works the room. Early on, I saw this was a big difference between us, but I thought I could live with it.

The winter after we got married, however, I was in for a bit of a shock. We had decided to spend a week in the Rockies skiing – just the two of us. We were really looking forward to spending this time together. As we headed out to the slopes on our very first day, we met some other couples in the hotel lobby. Immediately, Eric's attention was redirected. Instead of connecting with me, he was connecting with them. The magic of the moment was gone. Our romantic vacation became a networking event. I'm still upset about it. Even though I'm his wife, when we are in public, I feel like I have to fight for his attention.

This is Eric's take on the same incident:

ERIC: I'm an energetic, fun-loving people person. I like people – all kinds. That's what makes me such a successful salesperson. My wife Helene is very different...she has a delicate, pensive personality. Since our very first date, I have admired – and enjoyed – her serene and quiet energy. We complement each other really well.

For our first vacation, we went to the Rockies. That's when I had a rude awakening. We were spending time together, enjoying the atmosphere and each other. But we were staying in a hotel, and when you're in a public place, you're going to end up meeting people. I struck up a conversation with a couple, and Helene immediately felt that I had lost interest in her. Does she really need my undivided attention? We had spent a few wonderful hours alone. What's wrong with interacting with some fellow human beings? I'm starting to feel very claustrophobic.

When they dated, Helene was amused by Eric's outgoing, friendly nature. Eric was attracted to Helene's serenity and inwardness. Their mutual infatuation covered over the fact that their opposite natures would eventually challenge them in a serious way.

After that rude awakening in the Rockies, Helene and Eric traveled the downward spiral and spent an enormous amount of time resisting each other and trying to change each other. This approach only led to more misery, which is why they came to see me. How did they ultimately turn their marriage around? By rebuilding, step by step, using the upward spiral as their guide.

Everyone knows that marriage – like anything worthwhile in life – takes work. But we want to make sure that we are making the right efforts – efforts that will produce real gain. All too often, I've watched people make aimless efforts – the kind that lead to exhaustion and frustration because there is little (or zero) improvement in the relationship. Real success begins with the hands-on tools I'm going to outline.

When Helene and Eric had their rude awakening, they thought their marriage was in trouble and that they had made a terrible mistake. "Could I really have married someone so different from me?" "How can we ever make this work?" They had no idea that this obstacle was the beginning of something fantastic – that by learning about each other, they would develop an even deeper connection. Every rude awakening is really a crossroads. It can be the critical point where a relationship sinks into a downward spiral – or it can be the jumping-off point from which the marriage gets propelled up an upward spiral.

The following chapters will show you the steps that Helene and Eric succeeded in using to deepen their marriage and create a stronger bond than ever, *based on the differences* between them. You'll read about their specific process in chapter 9, "A Case Study Illustrating the Upward Spiral," but meanwhile, let's learn about the upward spiral toward positive change.

In the following chapters we will explore the three steps of the upward spiral in depth. We will learn how to use them to take the winning route to a dynamic relationship that not only embraces personality differences but actually uses them to maximize each partner's potential – as well as the team potential of any marriage.

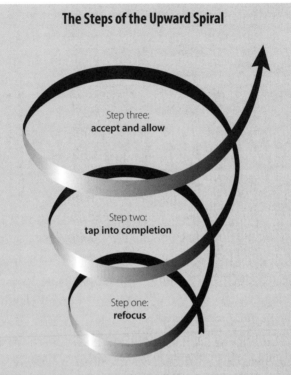

The Steps of the Upward Spiral

Step three:
accept and allow

Step two:
tap into completion

Step one:
refocus

STEP ONE: REFOCUS

In this stage you refocus on areas of easy, innate connection that serve as anchors in your relationship.

STEP TWO: TAP INTO COMPLETION

Here you see how your differences actually complete and complement each other and have the power to take you and your marriage to the next level.

STEP THREE: ACCEPT AND ALLOW

The clarity gained from refocus and completion opens the door to developing true acceptance, which is the gateway to respect – and true love.

Chapter 4

Step One: Refocus

One reason the downward spiral is so well traveled is that our brains have a natural negative bias. Brain research shows that the brain reacts much more strongly to negative stimuli than to positive. On one hand, this negative bias serves us by alerting us and accentuating possible dangerous situations. However, when it comes to relationships (and our own inner happiness), negative bias can wreak havoc. Psychologist Dr. Rick Hanson articulates this phenomenon succinctly: "Your brain is like Velcro for negative experiences and Teflon for positive ones."*

Because of this neurological negativity, our brains not only hyper-focus on the challenges accompanying our personality differences, but also minimize the easy, innate connection we have with our spouses in other areas. To correct this imbalance, this chapter will focus on three easy, basic areas of connection that are often taken for granted.

---

* Rick Hanson, PhD, *Buddha's Brain: The Practical Neuroscience of Happiness, Love, and Wisdom* (Oakland, CA: New Harbinger Publications, 2009), p. 41.

> **Invaluable Resources for a Strong Marriage**
>
> The following three areas of easy, innate connection are among your best marriage resources.
>
> - Similarities between spouses
> - Our spouses' virtues and assets
> - Our shared relationship history

I will refer to these three areas of easy, innate connection as "resources." As we proceed to look at all three, take notice of which of these resources you can relate to. It's entirely possible that you do not relate to any of these three examples. If this is the case, I suggest that you search your own marriage to find the unique resources that you have. Rest assured – they're there.

The exercises in this chapter are recommended for all spouses to do everyday – on good days as well as on challenging days. If you develop this habit, it will serve you well in all times. However, when dealing with personality differences, it is practically an imperative. This is why it's the first step of the upward spiral.

Resource 1: Similarities between Spouses

At this point, you might be wondering, if this book is about personality *differences,* why is there such an emphasis on *similarities* in this chapter? As I mentioned in chapter 1, both differences and similarities play their roles. We've seen that personality differences are essential. Although our similarities also played a huge role in the decision to marry a particular person, for most of us, it's our differences that *subconsciously* led us to tie the knot. Our similarities are a source of safety but at times, can become boring and monotonous. On the other hand, our differences create challenge – and excitement.

When we become overwhelmed by our differences, however –

whether they are differences in personality, values, or lifestyle – it can be unnerving. Similarities of any sort serve as a strong basis to lean on. Most couples have more in common than they think. Once these similarities are identified, they act as a solid foundation upon which a couple can dance with their differences. For one couple – Beth and Pete – this works as follows:

BETH: Our relationship runs very deep. The translation of our son's name into English is "calm." We share some sort of calm, a desire for a life of calm, a calm tone… We communicate on the same wavelength.

CHANA: Do you have differences in personality?

BETH: We have a lot. I am more take charge, vocal and loud. Pete does his thing quietly, without bells. He is more laid-back; he will achieve things quietly from an internally quiet place. He's also more patient and very focused. I need to work hard to motivate myself.

CHANA: How has that mutual calm in your personalities impacted your marriage?

BETH: When our pace clashes – and I feel annoyed – just remembering that we share this calm softens the negative feelings.

Somehow it is all too easy for a couple to overlook their similarities and other easy points for connection – particularly when they're overwhelmed by their differences. This is why it's so important to get specific about identifying your similarities.

Identifying *Your* Similarities

Significant similarities typically fall into one of the following categories:

- Personality similarities
- Values similarities
- Lifestyle similarities or similar interests

Personality Similarities

While many couples I interviewed (such as Beth and Pete) named
a strong similarity in personality traits, other happily married couples in the study could not think of *a single* personality similarity.

One guy I interviewed, Greg, said that it took a bit of time
before he saw his wife Cynthia's outgoing side. Although it wasn't
his initial connector, it was one of the strong connectors in his
marriage of eight years: "We're both 'people' people. I love that we
share this trait." Cynthia found a different personality similarity:
"The trait that most connects us is our shared sensitivity; we are
both connected to each other's feelings and think a lot about what
the other said or meant."

In my relationship study, these were the most common personality similarities:

cheerful	loving	trustworthy	hospitable	committed
patient	sensitive	competitive	playful	hardworking
open-minded	empathic	dependable	forgiving	respectful
compassionate	optimistic	spontaneous	gentle	creative
confident	honest	quirky	humorous	down-to-earth

Exercise for Personality Similarities

- Identify a common personality trait or traits that you and
  your spouse share.
- If it's hard to think of one, see if you can try a bit harder.
- If you don't find one at all, no worries – maybe this is not
  your category.

Values Similarities

During my research, when I asked various couples what their
personality similarities were, strangely enough, often the answer
was a value, not a personality trait. Consider this exchange:

CHANA: What is a *personality similarity* between you and your spouse?

SUSAN: Bob and I are both highly idealistic, we both really want the best. I know this is going to sound kind of corny but we both want the best for the world. We have a common vision of what a neighborhood and community is supposed to be; we want to see people unifying. We want to see people getting along, looking out for each other.

When I interviewed Bob separately, this is what he said:

BOB: We think in a similar way. For example, we both believe that life is for learning to be fair and kind to people, that life is service and that we're not simply here for ourselves. Our faith goes along with that and a common love of nature and a similar aesthetic.

Just like Susan and Bob, sometimes people mix up values and personality traits because they're not clear what exactly values are. To start, a value is a bedrock core belief. Although some of us have never analyzed or defined our values, they're there. A prime value is something we not only stand for – we would even fight for it because it is our core; it's who we are. Although we might not live up to this prime value, if we fell short, we would be very disappointed. This is the reason that radically different values pose the greatest threat to a marriage.

A couple does not need for *all* of their values to match up. If one, two, or three of their primary values match, a firm foundation can be established. I know of a couple who shares two values, no personality similarities, and zero interests, and they are happily married. Their common two values are: they are fully committed to their marital vows and they believe in giving. Besides this, they are complete opposites in every way. And they have a wonderful marriage.

There's a second reason people give examples of values when asked for personality similarities: there's usually a personality trait associated with a value. For example, if hard work is a value for someone, he or she will usually also have the personality trait of being a hard worker. If we share family values with our spouses, we usually also share the personality trait of loyalty or devotion.

When I culled the data from my relationship study, I found these to be the most common shared values:

kindness	teamwork	self-assurance	freedom of expression
morals	empathy	orderliness	fiscal responsibility
hard work	honesty	responsibility	personal integrity
calmness	education	trustworthiness	political affiliation
sensitivity	spirituality	privacy	communication
compassion	loyalty	love for life	environmentalism
religion	traditionalism	love of animals	personal growth
commitment	spontaneity	altruism	perseverance
generosity	forgiveness	healthy living	volunteering
optimism	dependability	efficacy	self-control
happiness	respectfulness	family-centered living	flexibility

Exercise for Values Similarities

Answer the following questions.

- Identify at least one common value that you and your spouse share.
- How has this (these) shared value(s) helped you feel more connected to your spouse?
- Is there a personality trait(s) that you share, that stems from this (these) shared value(s)?

Lifestyle Similarities or Similar Interests

Although similarities of interests and lifestyle (hobbies, social life, etc.) are not essential for a happy marriage, they are good resources because they can provide a comfort and "flow" in the relationship. For instance, Jon and Amy share a common lifestyle and interests – as Jon said, "It's great that we're both in computers; we have the same head. We actually studied in the same school. And we both love hiking." Amy shared, "We met in college; actually we used to do our homework together…that's how we bonded! And our long hikes were the icing on the cake."

Although Jon and Amy also shared a very strong value of family commitment, their initial connector was their shared lifestyle/ interests. They actually reminded me of a shared interest in my own marriage. My husband and I share very few personality traits in common. Although we do share values, we also have an absolute love of camping and the outdoors. Our annual campout week takes us right back to our dating days. It gives us and our marriage energy for months on end. Lifestyle similarities are not essential in a marriage, but if they're there, you can really cash in on them.

Here are a few examples of lifestyles/interests from my relationship study:

music	books	cooking	night life	love to eat
gardening	golf	love dogs	traveling	gambling
shopping	gym	camping	clothing style	antiques
sport events	rodeo	eating out	museums	rappelling
movies	comedy	past history	love cats	tennis

Exercise for Lifestyle Similarities

Do you and your spouse share any similarities in lifestyle or interests? This could include shared hobbies, interests, social activities, etc. Make a list.

If You're Having Trouble Identifying Similarities

Most couples have more similarities than they realize; it's essential to be aware of them. Here are some interesting similarities couples discovered and shared with us. Their insights might help you to uncover similarities from the above three categories that you share with your spouse.

PERSONALITY SIMILARITIES

- Although we have different interests, we both get into our interests intensely.
- We entertain ourselves differently, yet we both entertain ourselves, rather than rely on others to entertain us.
- We both need space and give this space to each other.
- We both enjoy being in close proximity to each other.

VALUES SIMILARITIES

- We can unite to keep divisive people (sometimes in-laws) from coming between us.
- We are both strong believers in our values, even if most of our values don't match up.
- We are both committed to marriage.
- We both believe in doing everything we can to avoid divorce.
- We both make mistakes and can say, "I'm sorry," although our styles of apology differ.
- We can both forgive.
- We can agree to disagree.

LIFESTYLE SIMILARITIES OR SIMILAR INTERESTS

- We like the same foods.
- We like different foods, but we really enjoy food.
- If we don't like many of the same things, then perhaps we share a dislike of the same things.

- We both like the apartment to be warm.
- We both like the apartment to be cool.
- We're both morning people.
- We're both night people.

Resource 2: Virtues and Assets in Your Spouse

Living day in and day out with someone makes it all too easy to overlook his or her virtues. A virtue is an attitude, disposition, or character trait that inspires us in a positive, moral way. When identifying your spouse's virtues, keep in mind that no one is 100 percent perfect. We all fall short of our standards on some level. However, getting in touch with your spouse's virtues engenders warm feelings of connection and appreciation.

Here are some examples of virtues to get you started:

accountability	empathy	idealism	protectiveness	self-made
commitment	faith	integrity	prudence	service
cooperation	forgiveness	justice	purposefulness	sincerity
honesty	flexibility	love	reliability	wisdom
courage	gratitude	modesty	resilience	tact
discretion	hope	peace	resourcefulness	tolerance

Resource 3: Shared Relationship History

For some couples, the strongest resource is their significant shared past.

Examples are:

- What we've been through together
- The storms we've weathered together
- The children we brought into this world together (or brought up together)
- The way we've changed and grown as individuals, together

- The way our marriage has improved (even though it might not be our ideal marriage)
- The good times we've shared together
- The times we were there for each other

Clearly, a shared past history is more of a resource for couples who have been together for a long time. This being said, even fairly young couples can find plenty of past shared experiences to bond over. For example, the planning of a wedding is both exciting and challenging. Looking back, this experience is typically filled with wonderful and happy memories, as well as trying ones that can serve as building blocks.

Everything a couple has come through together strengthens their "team" and can be used as a resource. When a couple reminisces about their shared victories and triumphs, they strengthen the foundational fibers of their relationship. This is a key for stability and connection.

The Tool of Refocus

Now that you have done the work of locating and defining your resources, you're ready for the tool of refocus. If we just intellectualize the information about our similarities, it won't necessarily change us – or our marriages. The purpose of refocus is to bring this knowledge to life. We need to take it in, think about it, and allow ourselves to rejuvenate those innate feelings of connection.

Think about it this way: A filmmaker skillfully shifts a viewer's focus back and forth by use of lights, camera angle, and so on. We too can shift focus within moments; instead of focusing on the annoying aspects of our spouses' personalities, we can choose to focus on the wonderful connectors. Again, it is human nature to focus on the negative. It definitely takes an effort to make this switch – which is why I'm spelling it out, in this book. But we can do it, and the reward is more than worth it.

"Instead of focusing on the annoying aspects of our spouses' personalities, we can choose to focus on the wonderful connectors."

Throughout the next few chapters, you'll see examples of people who truly impacted their marriages by refocusing.

Flex Your Refocus Muscles

Here are some exercises to help you access the power of refocus in your marriage.

- Review the resources that you share with your spouse. Make sure that they are crystal clear in your mind.

- Be hyper-aware of the times when your spouse exhibits these qualities. For best results, write these moments down.

- At every opportunity, make sure to express to your spouse how much you love or appreciate this behavior/trait/talent/feature about him or her.

Knowledge is power, especially in marriage. The more aware you are of your resources, the more you can make use of them – either as a way to hurdle over rough patches or just to draw even closer during good times.

Every marriage is like a tapestry. There are many threads, such as each partner's past experiences, family-of-origin stories, and similarities. Our resources serve as a firm foundation for our marriages. But the most essential threads – the threads that have the power to keep the fabric of the marriage strongly bound and to keep our relationships alive and dynamic – are our personality differences.

   With our resources in hand, we are now ready to learn how to dance with our differences.

Chapter 5

Step Two: Tap into Completion – Personal Balance

We've been talking about completion throughout this book; now we're ready to learn how to put it into action. When I interviewed Brett, he literally blew me away with his take on completion.

Vivian and Brett met in college, where Brett fell for Vivian almost immediately. Vivian, however, didn't exactly share the sentiment and continually brushed him off. Soft-spoken, mild-mannered Vivian was turned off by his "overly friendly," outgoing personality. For two years, Brett pursued and Vivian pushed away. Even after they graduated and returned to their hometowns, many thousands of miles away from each other, Brett didn't give up. He had seen something in Vivian that he could not forget. Deep inside, Brett felt that she was the woman he wanted to spend his life with.

So Brett continued to pursue Vivian through letters. For one whole year, he wrote her a letter every single day (by the way, this story took place about fifteen years before the movie *The Notebook*). Slowly, Brett's letters began to penetrate Vivian's heart as she got a glimpse into his soul. She was able to see his deeper, internal side, a side that had never come through in their college interactions.

It took a whole year for her to fully come around, but she did ... and twenty-three years later, they have a very beautiful, vibrant marriage. But their marriage took some serious work. You see, even though Brett knew for sure that he wanted to spend the rest of his life with Vivian, he didn't know how to spend day in and day out with someone so introverted and slow paced (he is very fast paced). In addition, Brett is a big spender, while Vivian is a saver.

How did Brett and Vivian work with their differences? "Marriage was great at first, until I discovered just how slow paced Vivian is. It was really frustrating," remembers Brett.

BRETT: I kept asking myself, 'How did I marry such a slow woman?' It took me a very long time. But then I started to notice *the strength in her slowness.*

I saw calmness in her; she was calm and content in whatever she was doing. My tendency to get easily frustrated and agitated never even fazed her. It was something interesting to me. It took me a few years to realize that it was definitely something to learn from. I am fast, quick, impulsive – she has saved me from making many mistakes over the years. So now I get it; her slowness balances me out.

Brett worked so hard to win Vivian over. His kids even have all those love letters saved in a special place, as an heirloom. And yet, Brett could have had a miserable marriage ... if he hadn't discovered the power of completion. But with those five words, "the strength in her slowness," he really *got* completion.

This is the power of completion. When Brett chose to look at his wife's "flaw" in a positive light – and saw how it balanced him out – he flipped on the light in his marriage. As a result, he was able to reconnect to the excitement and attraction he had felt early on in their relationship.

The Two Aspects of Completion in Marriage

- PERSONAL BALANCE. We can become more balanced, developed people through marriage, specifically because of our spouses' different personality traits.
- TEAMWORK/SYNERGY. Because of our complementary differences, our team potential is exponentially greater than our solo potential. (For more on this, see chapter 6, "Completion and the Ultimate Teamwork/Synergy.")

Our personality differences encourage us (and sometimes push us) to step out of our comfort zones to experience and try to understand the new perspectives and behaviors of our spouses. If we're into personal growth – and not just lip service – marriage is the ultimate opportunity for growth, specifically *because* our spouses have different personality traits.

"Marriage is the ultimate opportunity for growth, specifically *because* our spouses have different personality traits."

We all wish that marriage were easy – and that life were easy. Yet, simultaneously, we all want to grow. This is a contradiction in terms because we all know that growth isn't easy; it takes concerted effort and energy. This is why we all have a list of changes we'd sincerely like to make in ourselves. But with all of our sincerity, the list seems to fall by the wayside.

What is the gift of marriage? Marriage pushes us to grow – to see ourselves objectively and face the effect we have on others. But the bonus is that marriage pushes us to do this in the context of a caring and committed relationship. And the more we grow, the more we can love.*

Unfortunately, many couples lose the love – or never develop it – because they get stuck in the downward spiral (chapter 2). They don't know how to tap into the growth and completion inherent in their marriages. In other words, they never learn how to love with their personality differences.

I'm going to give you nine different ways to make sure that you can flip the completion light switch on – again and again – in your relationship. (Six switches will be explored in this chapter, three switches in chapter 6.)

Completion Switch #1: Looking Inward

During the first years of his marriage, Brett was, shall we say, less enamored of his wife's slowness; in fact, it drove him crazy. "I definitely spent time floundering in what you call the 'downward spiral.' I lost respect for Vivian. I tried to change her...and for sure compared her to my friends' wives," recalls Brett. "But all this did was to make me pull away from Vivian and feel sorry for myself. If I had continued down this path, I could have lost the love of my life."

Then he began to switch his focus from his wife to himself:

BRETT: The turnaround for me was when I started to pay attention to the many times that my fast, impulsive nature got me –and

---

* This is why the word for marriage in Hebrew is *nisuin*, which means "to grow or lift up."

my family – into trouble. I always thought that it was a great thing to be so energetic, but when I humbled myself a bit, the faultiness of my nature began to hit me in the face.

This realization allowed me to start seeing the strength in her slowness. When I was being critical of her, the positive side of her slowness just went right over my head. But once I looked at myself, I saw her strength crystal clear. Today, it is so clear that I can't imagine how I managed to miss it! But I guess that's what happens when you are stuck in negativity. Facing myself and realizing that I had my own stuff to work on saved me from walking away from my better half.

When Brett started to focus on his own issue with impulsivity, it became easier to see the strength in Vivian's slowness. Once he got the right perspective, he was actually relieved by the fact that she balanced him out. (You will hear Vivian's side of the story in chapter 8.)

This process of looking inward takes some effort – something most of us instinctively resist. But life teaches us that when we hang in there, as Brett did, we emerge more complete, as greater people.

One of the earliest sources of the concept of completion is in ancient Hebrew wisdom. From a Judaic perspective, a peaceful marriage is only attainable if the partners learn to see each other through the eyes of completion.

The completion perspective teaches us to stop focusing on our spouses' behavior (and what we believe they are doing wrong) and instead focus on ourselves (how we can improve and how our spouses are catalysts for us to become more complete as people). The more focused we are on the other, the more annoyed we become with his or her behavior. The way out of this negative cycle is to focus on our own personal growth.

Exercise for Completion Switch #1: The Power of Looking Inward

- Identify one personality difference between you and your spouse.
- Consider how this difference helps you and your spouse complement each other.
- Brainstorm and make a list of ways that the personality differences between you and your partner help you to become a better, more balanced person.

Completion Switch #2: The Initial Attraction

Remembering the initial attraction to your spouse – that you had in the early stage of your relationship – is an important way to refresh and revitalize your marriage. Therefore, we want to tap into the conscious or subconscious role our personality differences played in our initial attraction. Look for something your spouse has that you don't have or vice versa. Was this a catalyst for your initial attraction? This kind of attraction is often subconscious and therefore tends to be pushed off to the side. We want to bring it forward. Remember, the attraction generated by personality differences, if used properly, can be a source of continual attraction throughout one's marriage. Using the completion mindset allows us to make sense of our personality differences in a deep and profound way. This opens the door to accessing that initial unique attraction and continually reviving it.

For example, Erica called me in a state of panic; she was convinced that her son Spencer had married the wrong woman. This wasn't just a suspicion; Spencer had told her outright that he wasn't particularly happy in his new marriage. When I spoke to Spencer, I learned more. Growing up, Spencer and his mother enjoyed many intellectual conversations – Erica is a highly cerebral woman. Early in his marriage, Spencer, who is also highly cerebral, began to focus on the fact that he couldn't have these types of conversations with his wife.

As Spencer and I spoke, he admitted that when he was dating, he was drawn to Ashley's warm personality, social grace, and love for children. He had dated many intellectual women in his past, and the fit just wasn't right. In addition, although his childhood memories of his mother were generally good, he also remembered how she frequently left the house to pursue yet another university course or to attend a fascinating lecture. He wanted something different for his kids.

When he began remembering and focusing on what had first attracted him to his wife, Ashley – and the wisdom behind this attraction – Spencer started to step out of his unhappiness and reconnect to the strong attraction he felt toward Ashley, which had slowly started to fade. The completion mindset helped him discover that this attraction to an opposite is an alive, active, and vibrant source of connection. It can indeed act as superglue in keeping a marriage strong during challenging times, even if it was not part of the initial attraction.

Exercise for Completion Switch #2: The Initial Attraction

- Think back to when you met your spouse. What was the magnetic pull that first attracted you to him or her (besides physical attraction, which typically is a given)? Can you pinpoint a personality difference that was playing a role, even subconsciously?

- Write down how you felt; the more descriptive, the better. The secret to reviving emotional experiences is to write them down with as much emotionally descriptive detail as possible. This will be helpful to reawaken this feeling again and again throughout your marriage.

Completion Switch #3:
Freedom from Your Comfort Zone

Since life begins at the end of our comfort zones, personality differences present the perfect opportunity to stretch ourselves – and to actually start *living*!

When you were dating, do you remember being energized by the attraction to your partner? One of the main things – subconsciously – fueling your attraction was the desire and pull to step outside of your own comfort zone. For many people, it felt like an adventure; your heart and mind began to experience the other person's vision and approach to life. The world looked more exciting and colorful. This excitement was actually a promise: the promise of growth that we feel every time we step out of our comfort zones and experience a new dimension of being.

This venturing out of one's comfort zone is what led Dylan, one of the men in my relationship study, to date realists, even though he is the ultimate optimist. "I've had three serious relationships in my life, including my present wife. All three of these women are very strong, structured, grounded, and a bit pessimistic. The attraction happened before I noticed that the women were like this!"

No one ever says, "I'm looking for a pessimist." But underneath the surface, Dylan was looking for a type of grounded and structured personality that is often coupled with a more pessimistic view of life. This is what balanced his personality. So when he met his wife Andrea, there was a subconscious feeling of completion. He needed her structure and realism. Likewise, Andrea needed Dylan's optimism. As a result of their contrasting natures, they each developed a crucial part of themselves.

Once the honeymoon phase of a relationship is over, we tend to magnify the ways our partner isn't like us – even though those differences were what brought us together in the first place. This tendency is based on the belief that "If you're not like me, you're against me." Sometimes, our spouses' differences are seen as a form of betrayal. We wonder: "If my spouse is so different from me, can she really be my ally?" Personality differences can also be felt as rejection – one might think, "If he's outgoing and admires that trait, perhaps he's annoyed that I'm reserved."

The natural response to this dissonance is to try to change the other person. A little change is inevitable. For instance, over time, Dylan may help his wife judge more favorably; Andrea may help Dylan set more realistic goals. But if we expect dramatic changes from our spouses (and we are set on changing them), we're missing the whole point. The goal is not to become identical, but rather to learn from and complement each other ... *and to balance each other out.* (Is there ever a time to ask your spouse to change? I will answer this question in chapter 7.)

When personality differences create tension and frustration in a relationship, you have the opportunity to step out of your comfort zone. Instead of looking at your spouse's contrasting trait as negative, you can reframe it as the very thing that will propel you to personal greatness – as an individual and as a spouse.

Exercise for Completion Switch #3: Freedom from Your Comfort Zone

- Identify several ways that you have already grown and developed as a result of your personality differences. How have you already stretched yourself?

- Identify several ways that you can grow as a result of being married to your partner. How do your personality differences force you to stretch yourself?

Completion Switch #4: The Curiosity Cure

Nathaniel and Paula had a nice working marriage except for when their major personality clash surfaced. Paula was extremely organized, prompt, and had a sense of "appropriateness"; things should be put in their place and rules should be followed. When she met Nathaniel, she was very drawn to his creative, laid-back personality. He always seemed to be calm and collected, unlike Paula's ex-fiancé, who had fought with her constantly.

Once married, Paula found herself becoming increasingly annoyed by Nathaniel's "spaciness" which she had originally perceived as his "creative and flowing" personality. She would often yell at her husband when he did "spacey" things, such as losing the keys or forgetting to buy an item or two on the shopping list. Nathaniel became increasingly sensitive to Paula's yelling and endless demands that everything had to be put in its place. He labeled her as "overly fussy." She labeled him as "spacey." When the name-calling became a mainstay in their marriage, they decided to get some help.

In my first meeting with Paula and Nathaniel, I watched them spin their wheels, over and over again, as they took their positions: "I'm right, you're wrong." "You're overly fussy." "You're spacey." They were stuck in their roles. They both asked me, "How can we possibly grow close when we are so ridiculously different?"

When people are stuck in seeing "different" as bad, they shut down...and shut doors in their relationships. Things tend to spiral downward from there. Curiosity opens the door to seeing different just as different – without judgment. Curiosity invites exploration and intrigue, which then opens the door to seeing how each marriage partner can balance the other out. But it isn't easy to be curious about someone's behavior when you're annoyed!

Here is the secret formula for learning: the desire for knowledge precedes the acquisition of it. This is why the best students are typically the ones with the most questions. This applies to marriage as well. When we first meet our spouses, we usually want to know everything about them. Their worldview. Their opinions. What their childhood was like. Who their mentor is. What they do when they first wake up. After the wedding, if you stop asking questions about your spouse – about what drives him and makes him tick, why she acts the way she does, how his personality developed – you'll cut short your ability to really know him or her. And that deep, intimate knowledge of another person is what's at the root of real love.

For Paula, cultivating curiosity took some work. She remembers, "It was extremely difficult at first, but I caught on. I tried to be curious about creative people and actually googled a few biographies of some creative types. This opened my eyes and allowed me to see how creative people function and think. The more I explored and understood his world, the more his behavior started to make sense. For sure, my curiosity melted a lot of my annoyance."

When we look at our spouses' personality differences with curiosity instead of judgment, we are able to stand outside of ourselves, as observers. Curiosity is how children learn; that childlike wonderment is the beginning of all learning. Only when we feel curiosity can we begin to *explore* and truly appreciate our partners' unique intelligence.

Exercise for Completion Switch #4: The Curiosity Cure

- Identify one major personality difference between you and your spouse. Brainstorm ways that you can be more curious about this different trait.
- Pick an interest or hobby that your spouse has that you do

not share. Take a few minutes out of your week to read up on this hobby and to ask your spouse "curious questions" about this interest, such as "How do you feel when you're involved in this hobby? How has it added to your life?"

Completion Switch #5: Swapping Shoes

Curiosity really is a precursor to switching shoes; it's what enables you to switch perspectives and put yourself in your spouse's place. As Nathaniel described:

NATHANIEL: I worked hard and pushed myself to step out of my "creative" mindset and put myself in Paula's "organized" shoes. I started to understand that Paula was suffering every time I forgot to put things back in their place. Even though it was hard for me to relate to her strong reaction to my messiness, I realized that I didn't have to relate to it. I just needed to open my eyes to the pain I was causing her. Once I stopped focusing on my pain and focused instead on her pain, I naturally wanted to try harder to be more organized.

Paula was able to switch shoes when she started to see that Nathaniel really was suffering when she yelled at him. As she explained:

PAULA: It was amazing because I am personally not sensitive to raised tones of voice. I would sum up my relationship with my ex as a yelling match. In comparison, my raised tones with Nathaniel didn't even register [for me] as anything. But Nathaniel perceived me as yelling; I realized that for someone with his tranquil, sensitive personality, raised tones of speech are startling and unsettling.

When we're getting along, we can slip into our spouses' shoes willingly as we try to understand life through their perspective.

But when we're annoyed with our spouses, when their behavior makes us grimace, when we feel wronged, it can take a Herculean effort to see the situation through their eyes. There's a saying: "If you want to understand someone, walk a mile in his shoes. That way, you'll be a mile farther away from him...and...you'll have his shoes." We can all relate to this joke at difficult moments. However, putting ourselves in our spouses' shoes is one of the most important habits to cultivate.

By stepping into the other's shoes, Paula and Nathaniel found it easier to modify their behavior because they *really* understood that the other person was suffering. This allowed them to transform the very personality difference that was disconnecting them back into a source of connection. Again, this took effort...but it eased and improved their relationship considerably.

Anyone who has ever succeeded in stepping out of his or her own mindset and was brave enough to enter the other's shoes knows the awesome reward attached to this behavior. Besides an improved relationship, the personal empowerment that results from this type of expansion of oneself is tremendous. One of the most profound experiences in life is the expansion of self that we feel when we take the high road or stretch ourselves in a meaningful way. Very few things can equal the satisfaction and inner power we feel during these times. Although it is not easy to step out of our shoes and into another's, it can be a life-changing experience. Marriage provides daily opportunities for this awesome self-expansion.

Exercise for Completion Switch #5: Swapping Shoes

Think of one situation in which your spouse reacted in a different way than you did. Start to see the incident in the way that your spouse would see it, playing it through his or her eyes. (If you're not sure what this would look like, ask your spouse to walk you through the mindset.) Ask yourself the following questions:

- How can I make sense of what my spouse is doing, saying, or feeling?
- What could be the gain for my spouse in his or her behavior?
- What would it be like to live for two hours as my spouse, with those personality tendencies?

Completion Switch #6: Rejoicing in the Gift

In chapter 1, we saw how every positive character trait that we (and our spouses) bring into marriage is a gift ... that is typically accompanied by a challenge. At any given moment, we have the choice to focus on the gift or on the accompanying challenge. Paula learned to choose the gift: "When I stopped labeling Nathaniel as "spacey," I was able to see that this was the challenging side of his wonderful creativity. Then – naturally – my annoyance started to take a back seat. The more I work on this, the easier it gets. It's funny; Nathaniel has become a sort of role model of the calm I hope to develop in myself."

Likewise, Brett was able to see Vivian's gift of patience and groundedness very clearly when he chose to stop focusing on the challenge of her slowness. Instead, he was blown away when he discovered the "strength in her slowness." Dylan was surprised when he realized that he was consistently attracted to the "strong, structured, grounded – and somewhat pessimistic" type of woman. Once he understood the gift-challenge connection, he was able to choose to rejoice in his wife's gifts ... while graciously accepting the accompanying challenge of her "pessimism."

Adopting the completion mindset is, in one sense, the work of a single moment. It can take just a few seconds for us to reframe a situation and look at our spouses' flaws as an asset. The magic is all in our thought processes. But it can take years to develop the muscle to *continuously* adjust our lenses whenever we're faced with our spouses' conflicting personality traits. The more we practice, the easier it becomes. This is what University of Massachusetts psychology professor George Levinger was referring to when he said, "What counts in making a happy marriage is not so much how compatible you are, but how you deal with incompatibility."* A successful marriage, then, can be defined as one in which people are committed to flipping the completion switch on, again and again.

Exercise for Completion Switch #6: Rejoice in the Gift

- Identify one gift in your spouse's personality that you are no longer seeing, as a result of being focused on the challenge of this personality trait.
- Consider how your spouse can be a source of inspiration to you, as a result of your personality differences.
- Looking back on your relationship, identify when and how your spouse's personality differences have helped you, your marriage, and your children.

---

* Cited in Daniel Goleman, "Marriage: Research Reveals Ingredients of Happiness," *New York Times*, April 16, 1985, http://www.nytimes.com/1985/04/16/science/marriage-research-reveals-ingredients-of-happiness.html?pagewanted=all.

Chapter 6

Completion and the Ultimate Teamwork/Synergy

The next three completion switches deserve a chapter of their own because they focus on the teamwork aspect of completion, which is how couples expand from "me" to "we" thinking. A good team *blends* individual strengths so that they complement each other; this creates a wonderful synergy. When members of a team come together in camaraderie, toward a shared goal and vision, the sum is greater than the parts. As the saying goes, "Teamwork is the fuel that allows common people to attain uncommon results."

Completion Switch #7: Dividing (the Work) and Conquering (the Challenge)

Marriage is the ultimate team. At its best, teamwork maximizes strengths and brings out the best in each team member, which is why people in successful marriages don't just appreciate their spouses' differences – they take full advantage of them. When there's a project, each spouse plays the role that he or she is best suited for. With house hunting, for example, the quiet, intellectually driven wife will review all the contracts and necessary documents. The outgoing, people-smart husband will deal with the sales agents and hire all the inspectors. This is what I mean by the "synergy" of a team.

Natalie and Kevin are an example of a couple who learned to work as a team. They were attracted to each other *because* of the completion they experienced through their conscious personality differences. She was drawn to his organized, methodical, driven nature – he to her bubbly, upbeat personality. Despite this, their personality differences still became a challenge.

As Natalie explained, "I really liked the fact that Kevin was driven and always did things with a thought-out plan. But life has a pace of its own. Spontaneity is also necessary and helpful at times. When things didn't go according to plan, I felt that Kevin was always stunting the flow of things. Like if a neighbor suddenly needed something and popped over, he would get annoyed. When we had kids, it was especially obvious that Kevin couldn't roll with the punches. He couldn't handle when things got out of control. He would try to take over but I think that he created more chaos; he just doesn't know how to deal with kids." Natalie was struggling with her marriage.

Kevin was also struggling. He told me about their first interactions and how he had loved Natalie's vitality from the get-go. "It brought out a certain happiness in me that had always been locked away. I found myself laughing more, and there was a spring in my step. I felt so fortunate to have Natalie on board," he said. "But when we got married, her 'chilled-out' personality translated into her socializing a lot with neighbors and the house being a mess. And I noticed how spacey she is. Like when she would leave the house, she always, and I mean *always*, forgot something and would have to come back."

Natalie and Kevin hit a wall. But they were able to get their marriage back on track by applying the first two steps of the upward spiral. This is what their process looked like:

1. REFOCUS. Natalie and Kevin wrote and reviewed their unique relationship history. They had been through a lot together; their perseverance was special to them. Another resource was their shared value of spiritual growth. They honed the tool of refocus by writing down and reviewing these resources.

2. TAP INTO COMPLETION. Since Natalie and Kevin kept emphasizing how the "other" was wrong, we started with completion switch #1, looking inward. They each chose one thing to work on, in themselves. Kevin decided that he needed to learn how to be more patient with his little kids, who were constantly pushing his buttons. Toward this goal, he decided to speak to an expert in child education. Natalie said that she would spend twenty minutes a day organizing the house, even though it was her least favorite thing to do.

As they stopped complaining about – and working against – each other, Natalie and Kevin were ready to explore their team potential. A good team recognizes each player's individual strengths and learns to leverage them. So Kevin and Natalie started to make a list of their strengths. Natalie was graced with social skills, creativity, spontaneity, and patience with people and children, among other things. Kevin's strengths included organization, focus, ability to plan, and a good business mind.

"A good team recognizes each player's individual strengths and learns to leverage them."

When it comes to teamwork, if we expect each team member to have the same strengths we do, we get easily frustrated. This is why dividing and conquering is so important. How did this team divide their tasks to maximize their team potential?

NATALIE

- Took charge of their social agenda and was responsible for maintaining a good relationship with the neighbors and children's teachers (which Kevin came to appreciate in a big way).
- Held down the home front. As an artist, she was able to be more flexible with her schedule. Therefore, if someone needed to be in the house for mail delivery, construction, or whatnot, she was able to be there. In addition, she could stay home and care for a sick child if needed.
- Ran the carpooling and extracurricular activities for the kids.

KEVIN

- Took responsibility for paying the bills.
- Took care of all the grocery shopping for the family.
- Planned the family vacations, after Natalie came up with the general idea of what would be good for their kids' development.

Instead of undermining each other, Natalie and Kevin began to empower each other. Their kids also gained from being on a winning team: Natalie became a strong role model of inner joy, creativity, spontaneity, and social grace, while Kevin became an inspirational example of focus, ambition, and planning for his kids.

Every couple is a team. Just as the right hand can reach places the left hand cannot, every couple has "team potential" that is greater than the sum of its parts.

Exercise for Completion Switch #7: Dividing and Conquering

- Consider how you and your spouse divide up your roles, based on your personality differences.
- Identify a different type of contribution you would like to make, based on your personality strengths.
- Identify several things your spouse does that you don't like to do or know how to do. Express gratitude to your spouse for doing these things.

Completion Switch #8: Celebrating Your Team Victories

Often, we confuse sameness with closeness. We get trapped in the mindset of "If only my spouse were more like me, we could really be close." Although similarities are important, differences are essential because they are the primary way in which we learn. When we appreciate each other's differences, we can *celebrate* the many ways we successfully work together as a team. This type of celebration gives life and vitality to a marriage. Hillary and Jason exemplify this.

HILLARY: Aside from our values, Jason and I have very little in common. I'm a super active doer; my husband is a less active "be-er." I'm a confrontational person; he's not. I'm an extrovert; he's an introvert. The first years of our marriage, we had a tough time accepting each other with our differences. Today, it doesn't bother me at all...as a matter of fact, I enjoy it. We each have our roles, based on our personality strengths and weaknesses, and it really works for us. I enjoy the team we've created. I think we're a great couple!

JASON: I totally agree. For example, Hillary's assertiveness compensates for my weakness in this area. I hate confrontations with a passion... so, usually, in our lives, she'll handle the confrontations. I guess you can say that she lets me off the hook and keeps us from getting stepped on. Another difference is that I'm more of a touchy-feely kind of person; physical affection is important to me. I'll often be the one that's cuddling with the kids, giving the kids hugs. This is a tremendous benefit of our personality differences – we each give our family distinct things. I love this about our marriage.

Amy and Jon also celebrate their team victories:

JON: One thing I used to struggle with in Amy is her tendency to spend. She definitely buys a lot more than I am comfortable with... but I see her really trying to curb her spending tendencies, and I appreciate it because I know how hard it must be for her.

I really try to focus on the many ways Amy has enriched my life. Around new people, it's easier for Amy. I often feel uncomfortable in these social settings; she makes it easier for me in many situations. This is one of the things that first attracted me to her – that she's so active, always blogging and networking... she's a social woman. I really like it; we have a great social life as a couple because of Amy. I actually enjoy going out and socializing now, because of her. If you knew me before I got married, you'd say that this is nothing short of a miracle. I see her as our social ambassador; it's really cool to have someone like her by my side.

What does Amy have to say about all of this?

AMY: Jon can get pretty uptight at times, but he has become more relaxed and calm. I naturally have an easier time accepting things; I'm more optimistic and comfortable with messiness, with the kids as well. I definitely add a lot of color to our marriage!

When it comes to money, Jon's a big saver; I think it comes along with his organized nature. Most of our arguments were because of finances: I wanted to buy something, and he would say, "Let's save the money to buy an apartment." He is very careful. At first it bothered me when he would say, "Let's borrow from someone or use something old…we have to save for the kids' college education." My response would be, "Now…for college? I want this now!" But with time, I've come to appreciate the benefits of saving.

Today, I can do bigger things because we saved the money. It's been hard but it's really worth it to save, not only for the sake of our kids but for our own future as well. I just keep focusing on our growing bank account…and I smile from ear to ear. I was never able to save before; it's pretty cool that we're doing this!

You'll notice that Hillary and Jason, as well as Amy and Jon, replay in their minds their marital "victories" – all the things they can do together as a team that they were not able to do before marriage. "Completion thinking" helps rewire the brain – instead of fixating on the frustrating part of your spouse's personality, your brain automatically sends you in the opposite direction, to see the benefits of your spouse's personality difference. The first step is *noticing* all the victories and benefits; the second step is to hit replay and review them constantly.

**Exercise for Completion Switch #8:
Celebrating Your Team Victories**

- Identify one way in which you and your partner have worked together as a team in the past.
- Instead of just acknowledging this, celebrate it! Replay your marital victories in your mind. This kind of replay is invigorating!
- Imagine one new way you and your partner might be able to work together as a team in the future.

Completion Switch # 9: Enabling Greatness

If you really want to get the most out of your teamhood, look at your spouse as a role model for things you would like to develop in yourself. This is one of the perks of marrying someone different from ourselves; he or she will automatically have strengths that we lack. Sarah and Jake made this work for their team.

SARAH: What made me want to marry Jake was his resolve and ambition. He had a list of things he wanted to do in his life, and though he didn't have much experience, he tried and succeeded in accomplishing them. I also wanted to be this way. When we got married, he encouraged me to pursue my goals. Jake immediately saw that I had the talents but that I didn't push myself to try. He said, "Get out there, try this, try that... you can do it." And in the end, I tried and succeeded.

Jake has helped me build myself a lot, a lot, a lot. Sometimes you want to do something, but it's hard. In the beginning, I would say to him, "What? I can't do it!" Even though I wanted to do it, I didn't think I could succeed. We didn't have higher education; we had to teach ourselves. We didn't sit in university; we did it alone. I feel that when one person really helps a second, the second also wants to help the first to succeed. Each spouse has something to offer. I need his drive and ambition, and he needs my inwardness and groundedness.

Jake and Sarah's marriage illustrates the type of change that happens in an organic, healthy, and encouraging way, not through someone trying to change his or her spouse out of annoyance.

As Jake explained:

JAKE: When I met Sarah, she taught children, which is beautiful. But I did feel that she could do more. I travel around and teach; my hope was that she might partner up with me. In the end, we have lived in many countries, traveled to places far and wide. We succeed because we have different strengths. For example, I like to write; my wife speaks but doesn't write. She has become quite an influential speaker over the years. I have to admit that I'm very, very proud of her. Even though we're on the same path, we do it in a different way. In the beginning, she was afraid that she wouldn't succeed, but I saw that she had the special abilities to reach a greater public. She has a charm. People really like her; it's the way she speaks, the way she smiles. I'm much more of a dry type of person.

It's funny, we are very different people. We've had our share of tough times but in the end, all of our differences bring us together. I think this is what love is. This is what understanding each other is all about. Each of us is born with different abilities, in a different environment. I think that it's God's plan that a home functions in this way. At the end of the day, we complete each other. That's why after thirty years of marriage, even though I know that we're so different, sometimes it's hard to find the differences.

When I interviewed couples on five different continents, I was struck again and again at the unique fabric of each and every team. But the thing that most impacted me was to see how the couples who were successful in dealing with their personality differences used similar techniques. Once a couple realizes that marriage is a system, they start to see how each partner can help the other to grow as an individual and as a team.

Exercise for Completion Switch #9: Enabling Greatness

- Identify several ways that you can be a source of inspiration and encouragement to your partner (without looking to change him or her!) as a result of your personality differences.
- Identify a way that you can be a source of support to help enable your spouse to attain his or her goals and dreams. Break this down into simple steps and begin implementing your plan to support your spouse.

Chapter 7

Step Three: Accept and Allow Your Spouse's Nature

Many couples tell me that although they love each other, they have "fallen out of like." Refocus and completion are essential tools for preventing this fall, or for getting back into "like" and "love." But this "flow" is all too often interrupted by our tendency to be judgmental and negative – especially when we feel misunderstood or hurt. This negativity blinds us from seeing the completion. As a result, we can get stuck again, focusing on the challenges that accompany our spouses' gifts.

This is where acceptance comes in. Accept and allow is the tool that clears away the negativity and creates a new type of ease in the relationship so that the love can continue to flow. Trevor, one of the men in my relationship study, was lucky enough to discover the power of acceptance before it was too late.

Trevor told me about the low point he hit in his marriage. After spending years trying to change his wife – with zero success – he was one step away from divorce. He had already moved out; the divorce proceedings were put into action. But by the time I met him, his marriage was on the upswing.

What changed?

"A lot of people don't get it," he told me. "They think that if their spouses are different, they have to change them according to their 'recipe,' without understanding that it's not going to work. This is what I tried to do with my wife – to make her faster, more optimistic, more easygoing. But by force, with criticism, it doesn't work. Instead of change, I got anger and hatred."

As we were talking, I spelled out to Trevor the process of the downward spiral: People focus on differences, get turned off, try to change their spouses, compare and/or compete, live parallel lives and/or sink into contempt and/or hatred. When he heard this, his eyes grew wide and he said, "This is *exactly* what happened to me!" He continued:

TREVOR: You know, people run to get divorced. OK, so you remarry a different person, but who said it's going to be better with her? Who said that it's going to be easier for you? Who said that she will be a better match than this woman that you've built a home and family with for twenty years? I mean, everyone's got baggage. Your wife will bring hers; it's the same stuff in different shoes. So if you'll have to compromise here, you'll also have to compromise there.

Once I realized that I would have to work hard on a new marriage, I decided that I should first put the work into my current marriage. I remembered the time that we did renovations; I was in such a rush to get the job done that I bulldozed over my wife, who was telling me that I was cutting corners. Sure enough, because of my haste, the renovations were a flop and we had to start over. I started to think about the many ways that she is good for me. And I just tried to accept her, instead of fighting against all of the things that drove me up the wall. The more I accepted her, the more things started to turn around for me, and for us. Today, I look back at those hard times and I can't believe it was us. We're in such a different place. I *really* enjoy her company now, and it's only getting better.

True to Trevor's experience, often, only when we let go of trying to change and control do things start to fall into place.

If My Partner Would Just Change, We'd Be Fine!

Many of us understand, on a theoretical level, the importance of accepting our spouses as they are. But, emotionally, our entire being might resist it, thinking, "I'm afraid he'll never change if I accept him as he is!" or, "If I accept her, she'll just keep doing the same annoying things!" We tend to think that if we get upset enough at our spouses, they will somehow get the hint and become the way we want them to be. But the more we resist the way someone is, the more that person resists our resistance and becomes increasingly set in his or her ways.

Although most of us would agree in principle that it's not wise to try to change our partners, we still try (whether we're aware of it or not). Here's an interview with Lindsey, one of the women in my relationship study. She is a laid-back, fun, disorganized person who is married to a super responsible, organized, sometimes pedantic man.

CHANA: So, Lindsey, have you ever made an effort to change your husband?

LINDSEY: Not change him, just have him be a little lighter.

CHANA: That's not changing him?

LINDSEY: Oh, it is changing him. He can be so dark, I just try to lighten him up a little.

CHANA: Have your efforts to lighten him up been direct?

LINDSEY: Well, I think you have to use all the tactics.

CHANA: Have you gotten results?

LINDSEY: I think we've both come toward each other a little bit... maybe just a bit. I hope so.

CHANA: And that's a result of trying to change him?

LINDSEY: I look at it more like getting him to see the right way... not changing the person. "Changing" sounds bad.

CHANA: But what if both people think *their* way is right?

LINDSEY: Yeah, then that's changing. Yeah, I guess it's more like enlightening.

CHANA: Enlightening each other? How is that different from changing?

LINDSEY: It's not. It just sounds better, less harsh.

At the end of this conversation, Lindsey and I both started laughing. What struck me was that she had verbalized so clearly the thought process so many of us have, when we justify our attempts to change our spouses.

How can we break out of this relationship-damaging (and often futile) habit? We have to ask ourselves this question: How do *I* feel when someone tries to change me? We certainly do *not* feel like changing. We become defensive and resistant... and end up being more judgmental and critical toward that person. So we shouldn't be surprised when our partners get hurt and defensive and typically attack back or withdraw.

Trying to get our spouses to change in effect makes us dependent on them. That's because when we are on hold waiting for others to change, we put the success of our relationship – and our own personal happiness – in their hands. This, in effect, renders us powerless. Getting hung up on what our spouses are doing wrong is also a distraction and escape from one of marriage's true goals: to grow into the best version of ourselves possible. The irony, of course, is that when we accept our spouses and allow them to be who they are, this is when they are most apt to change (if our acceptance is authentic).

Of course, accept and allow is *not* meant to be exercised in an abusive relationship. It is essential to demand change if there is any sort of behavior that is out of bounds. I will discuss this more in depth below.

"Accept and Allow": What Do These Words Really Mean?

The words *accept* and *allow* mean to internally agree to a given reality, to let go and let a person be. Although accept and allow is an internal process, when a person truly lets go internally, people on the outside are affected in a meaningful way.

Here is what acceptance looks like:

- I see my spouse as a valid, different person, even with his or her faults.
- I see our relationship as valid and unique, even with the imperfections it contains.
- I can control my urge to change him or her into the "perfect spouse."
- I acknowledge daily the ways my spouse is putting up with me, my imperfections, and the ways I am so different from him or her.

Acceptance is not approval. Acceptance doesn't even mean that you agree with the person. Acceptance means that you accept a person for who he or she is. And when you accept, you don't expend energy fighting the issue at hand. Instead of fighting, you use the energy to deal with what is. Just as you can accept the weather, so, too, you can accept your spouse's difference. Resistance only depletes your energy. But also, as they say, what you resist persists.

When you give up your demands for how someone should be and make peace with the way he or she is, you create the space to "allow" that person to be– which is like saying, "I give you full permission to be the way you are." Of course, our spouses don't need our permission to be. But on some level, we subconsciously feel a right to protest the way our spouses are, thereby not giving them the space needed to be themselves. Allowing releases this block and grants the "right to be." This doesn't mean that you identify with your spouse's behavior. It does mean that you are internally letting go and letting him or her be. When this is done *sincerely* (*not* as a tactic), it is likely that your spouse will "get it," on some level.

When I think about the power of accept and allow, Grace's story comes to mind. She stepped into my office at a moment of tremendous frustration. Grace was going through a major internal struggle, and although her friends were there for her, her husband Jimmy was unable to fathom the emotional complexity of her challenge. I could see that she was sinking into the downward spiral. Her first complaint to me was, "All of my friends' husbands can give them emotional support; why can't mine? What was I thinking when I married him?"

When Grace calmed down a bit, I asked her – out of curiosity – what originally drew her to Jimmy. She was able to recall the outrageous attraction she had to his strong, disciplined, responsible character (here Grace employed the tool of refocus, of seeing a virtue). She felt really safe and protected with him, something she hadn't felt with the other men she dated (who happened to be on the more emotional side).

After Grace admitted this, she laughed out loud. "OK, I see where you're going with this," she said. "I knew, in my heart of hearts, that I needed to marry the tough guy. It's funny – a coworker told me the other day about her husband, who woke her up in the middle of the night because he found a rat in the apartment. He was scared. I remember thinking to myself, 'If Jimmy found a rat in the apartment, he'd know what to do. I would feel so safe; he would know how to take that rat on!'"

Grace and I spent the rest of the session discussing the power of accept and allow. When Grace went home that day, she looked at her husband with a renewed adoration; she thought to herself, "Yup, that's my rat fighter...he can get me out of any mess."

At our next session, Grace told me that the strangest thing happened:

GRACE: As I let go of my need for Jimmy to be this emotionally savvy type of guy, I guess I just "allowed" him to be who he really is – as you would put it. Then, a couple of days later, he noticed that I had trouble sleeping and asked me what was going on. I said, "You know...on one hand, I wish I could tell you...but then I'll get frustrated because you can't give me the emotional support I need. And it's OK; I know that's *not* why I married you. So, maybe it's better that we don't talk about it." Jimmy suggested that we should talk and that he would try to be there for me. After I shared my story, he said, "You know, I really don't know what to say...or how to help you. But what I can do is give you a hug."

And *that* was the best hug I ever got in my life. It was a five-minute hug...without words...but he was totally with me and supporting me, without saying a word. That was all I really needed.

"It's so true!" Grace said. "Only when I *accepted* who Jimmy is...

and *let go* of needing him to be that emotionally savvy guy was he able to be emotionally supportive of me – but in *his* way." (Notice: Grace didn't announce to Jimmy that she was going to accept and allow him to be. She just did it, and because it was authentic, he picked it up.)

Accept and allow actually frees your spouse to be who he or she is – and frees *yourself* from the shackles of your *expectations* of and resistance to your spouse. Everyone goes into marriage with expectations. But sometimes, we are so focused on our expectations that we don't really see the other person. We get angry and disappointed when our spouses don't live up to the expectations that we have.

One way to check our expectations is to ask ourselves a few sobering questions: Is this something that my spouse really needs to change, or can *I* change my expectations? Is this thing I think I need from my spouse really a requirement, or can I fulfill the need myself? Is it really my spouse's job to live up to my expectations?

It is absolutely exhausting to resist someone. When we release the resistance, we create an environment of cooperation and support (which alone can lead your spouse to change behavior). At the very least, accept and allow takes us out of the mode of reacting and puts us in a place of choice, which is always empowering.

What if – despite sincere effort – you're still struggling to accept your spouse? Sometimes, we need to look inward: if we have trouble accepting ourselves with our inadequacies, we tend to have trouble accepting other people with their shortcomings.

On a personal level, self-acceptance means loving ourselves and giving ourselves the freedom to be who we are. This doesn't mean that we gloss over or ignore our deficiencies. It doesn't mean that we don't work consistently on our shortcomings. However, our prime enemy is often our inner critic. And when the inner critic gets hold of us, our negativity tends to spill out on those closest to us. The flip side is that when we learn to forgive ourselves, we can learn to forgive others. This creates the ultimate environment for growth, for ourselves and our spouses.

Allowing is what happens when we give ourselves permission to be who we are, trust our instincts and intuition, and allow ourselves to make the choices that we need and want to make. In addition, the more content we are as individuals, the less needy we will be in our marriages. We really are capable of fulfilling many of our own needs. We've all been culturally primed to assume that the role of a spouse is to be our "everything." This flawed expectation leads to disappointment, anger, and the whole downward spiral. The more we are able to take responsibility for self-love and acceptance, the more we take the pressure off of the marriage.

Is There Ever a Time to Ask for Change?

Do we just have to accept *everything* in our spouses? A very important caveat as I mentioned above is that the technique of accept and allow is not meant to be exercised in an abusive relationship. If someone's behavior is out of bounds, such as objectively abusive behavior or unchecked addictions, *change is a necessity*. We can and should insist on change. It's essential to clearly communicate what behavior we can live with – and what behavior we absolutely will not accept.

"If someone's behavior is out of bounds, such as objectively abusive behavior or unchecked addictions, *change is a necessity*."

But let's talk about ordinary day-to-day situations that do not fall into the category of abuse. Regular situations are tricky because every spouse at times feels or thinks, "My spouse's behavior is intolerable." And yet, that behavior becomes tolerable once we learn to stretch...and remember that our spouses are also dealing with our "intolerable" stuff. However, if your spouse is doing something that's very difficult for you, either in frequency or intensity, a request might be appropriate. However, there are some important conditions for a successful request:

- GENERAL ACCEPTANCE. Do I accept my spouse for who he or she is? A request for change will likely fall on deaf ears, if I don't accept my spouse (in a general sense).
- SPECIFIC, NOT GLOBAL. Does my request address a specific behavior – and not a complete change of character?
- MUTUALITY. Am I open to making an equally challenging change in myself?
- INFREQUENT. Am I picking my battles? The more frequent my requests, the less chance that they will reap any benefits.

Here's an example of the *wrong* way to ask for change: "How many times have we been late because you couldn't find your phone... or wallet...or keys? You never organize anything. Your desk is a mess, your closet is a mess, your car is a mess. Can't you pull it together, already?"

This "request" is really an attack; it's as if the speaker is saying, "Just be organized like me. What's your problem?"

Here's what a productive request might sound like: "I really enjoy your creativity *and understand that it doesn't exactly go hand in hand with organization.* And thank you for agreeing to take the kids to school, every morning; it makes my life a lot easier. **I'm concerned at the moment because** the kids have arrived a bit late to school the last three days. *I know that being on time isn't something that comes effortlessly to you,* but **it is really important to me.** Can we put our heads together and see what can be done about this? I know that you care about the kids as much as I do *and that we care in different ways.* But **this is very important to me.**"

It takes more effort to craft this kind of request, but it's far more effective and productive. Note that this request acknowledges the personality difference yet asks for a specific change in behavior.

One reason this request is productive is because it uses many ingredients of a successful delivery, such as:

- TONE. The request is expressed with an air of acceptance and respect, not authoritatively or as a demand.
- TIMING. In moments of stress, open communication is more difficult. It's important to discuss major issues when the stress levels are down.
- EMPATHY. Taking the time to consider what the other person is going through and why they behave the way they do (see italics in example above).
- "I" LANGUAGE. No matter how emotionally mature we are, "you" language puts us on the defense. Instead of *"You* speak to me with an edge," try *"I* am sensitive to raised tones of voice. Is it possible for you to say the same message in a softer way?" (See bold print in example above.)
- THE SANDWICH. For excellent communication, sandwich your message between two sincere and specific compliments (see above example, underlined). The sandwich is an essential communication tool. When we sandwich our requests between two compliments, combined with "I" language, this is the winning combination.

If your spouse is able to go along with your request, make sure to show your gratitude in a big way! But generally, we want to save "change requests" for rare occasions and practice accept and allow consistently throughout our marriages. Real, lasting change happens in marriage in an environment of acceptance and love. When someone is breathing down our necks, the last thing we want to do is change. When we feel loved and accepted for who we essentially are, we're more likely to want to change.

Gary, one man I interviewed, teaches us this lesson beautifully. He struggled with his wife's tendency to be "highly stressed." Gary explained:

GARY: In the beginning, I definitely set out to change Rebecca. Given that stress is something that can kill you, it's better to take a deep breath and let go. But then I started to think about my parents' marriage and how my parents always tried to change each other...I hated it. So instead of trying to change her, I tried to support her – by attempting to help her through her stress. I guess I tried to model a different way of being, hoping she'd catch on. As a result, I think she's been trying to change herself. I'd say, within the last two years, I see a big difference.

Gary authentically wanted to help Rebecca improve her life. But even with his best intentions, had he been forceful or judgmental, I highly doubt that Rebecca would have been open to his suggestions and influence. He seems to have done a pretty good job; this is what Rebecca had to say:

REBECCA: Being around Gary definitely chills me out, and honestly I think that it's really a good match as far as that's concerned. In the beginning, I thought, "He's just going to have to 'get' the way I am, or this won't work." Our upbringing was so different as far as planning and perfectionism are concerned. In my family, we're all intense, stressed-out planners. We like to do everything just so. His family is more similar to him – they are very laid-back.

But Gary didn't yell at me and tell me to chill out. He watched me come back from work every day incredibly stressed out. Although he also had a stressful job, he knew how to unwind at home. Admittedly, I was pretty envious of his ability to do this. The contrast between the two of us became more and more glaring, and for sure, this is what prompted me to change. But what really made the difference was that he really, really cared about me. It wasn't about his ego; it was about him caring. I think that this is why I was so open to his influence. I decided that I had to learn to chill out, for my good and for the good of our marriage and future kids.

Last spring, it was so crazy and hectic at work that I was ready to give up teaching entirely. Gary was supportive of me doing whatever I thought best, but he also encouraged me to stick with it and focus on reducing some of the things that were stressing me out. Because of him, I didn't abandon a career that I love. Sometimes I imagine Gary as a mini person on my shoulder whispering in my ear, "RELAX, it's not a big deal."

As I mentioned in chapter 2, although we cannot change our spouses, we can be the reason for them to change. One way to do this is to model the behavior, as Gary did. But over the years, I have become convinced that the *most* effective way to help our partners to change is simply to change ourselves. When our partners see us making serious changes in ourselves in a consistent way, they often feel obliged to start making changes within themselves.

How Do I Know if It's Healthy?

Accepting and allowing are mature actions that come from strength and choice. These mature actions have nothing to do with the martyrdom syndrome (otherwise known as "victim complex"). A martyr is a self-appointed "victim" who puts other people's needs above his or her own so that he or she can suffer for the sake of others. This gives the martyr's life meaning; typically, martyrs expect to be showered with affection because of their sacrifices. Accept and allow is not about suffering; it's about choosing the higher road, from a place of strength.

If we fall into martyr mode, we cannot grow and evolve, because martyrdom equals powerlessness. Accept and allow is the epitome of *empowerment*. If chosen from a place of strength, accept and allow won't lead you to function in the role of an enabler – or to be a victim of humiliation, intimidation, or abuse.

Telling Signs of a Martyr

Here are some signs exhibited by people who are stuck in martyr mode:

- Stays in an abusive relationship and believes that he or she can change the abuser by behaving unselfishly.
- Frequently talks about how difficult life is because he or she has to sacrifice for others.
- Expects the person for whom he or she sacrifices to be involved in the minutiae of his or her life.
- Praises him- or herself highly as someone who chose to suffer for a noble cause.
- *Expects* sympathy but *refuses* assistance.

  If you are unclear as to whether you are in martyr mode or simply practicing accept and allow, it is best to speak to a trained professional to help you assess your emotional responses. This might be a necessary step to help you to access your inner strength.

Times of Stress

The most crucial time for accept and allow is during times of stress, because any stressor – positive *or* negative – can magnify personality differences. It could be a new baby, a change in one's job or job status, family events, or a move. If we're not more forgiving and accepting during stressful times, we can become the direct or indirect cause of more stress in the marriage. It helps to remind ourselves, as soon as a stressor appears in our lives, to expect for our personality differences to become more pronounced and to be aware that this could bring more frustration. If we do not succeed in being more forgiving *during* these times, then we might need to work hard at being more forgiving *after* these stressful times. Otherwise, the aftermath can cause lingering damage.

Chapter 8

Accept and Allow in Action – Making It Real

One of my more memorable radio interviews for my first book, *I Only Want to Get Married Once*, was with WCBS Radio talk show host Pat Farnack. When I mentioned that my next book would focus on strategies to help couples work with their personality differences, she asked to hear more. Of the techniques I shared, the one that most captivated her was accept and allow. I explained that when we let go and allow our spouses to be who they are, something special happens. There's a shift in the relationship, and we're able to push through to a whole new level in the marriage. Her response summed up the power of this technique: "That is so amazing! Accept and allow. *That says it all.*"

But, as I clarified to her, we can't do it in one shot. Accept and allow is a process. Here are seven tactics to help you make that incredible shift in your marriage.

Accept and Allow Tactic #1: Search for Good Intent

Evan, one of the men in my relationship study, shared his story:

EVAN: One big difference between Renee and me is that she
vacillates a lot; she has a yo-yo personality. She changes her
mind a lot – she's back to the original decision and then she
changes her mind again… where I'm like, "This is the decision,
let's do it and get it done."

I first noticed this difference when we had to buy a sofa. I
found the couch, I did a lot of research, the price was right. She
was like, "Hmm… do you want something else… no… so then
this is the couch… no… I don't know." In the end, she gave in,
but the process was very annoying for me.

Renee's procrastinating used to *really* bother me. I often felt
myself growling internally. It took me a while to realize that
there's an upside to Renee's procrastination. Her hesitancy
often stems from the fact that she cares so much and she's so
responsible – and I benefit from her caring in other ways, as
do our kids. This has definitely helped me accept and leave the
issue alone, instead of getting upset. I do this with many things.
Like, if we lose a deal because she took too long to decide, now
I say, "Well, we lost money on that but you weren't ready to
move forward. But it's not the end of the world." I'm not going
to fight about it now. And these days, it's more like she's learning
from these incidents… instead of me shoving them in her face.

Just because someone doesn't love us the way we want to be loved,
it doesn't mean that person doesn't love us with all he or she has.
We have a tendency to read negative intentions into our spouses'
behavior, particularly regarding a personality difference. That's
why it's extremely important to cultivate the habit of searching
for good intent.

Exercise: Search for Good Intent

- What would happen if you assumed that your partner was doing the best he or she could, considering his or her nature?
- Instead of deciding that your spouse is doing _____ (fill in the blank) on purpose, ask yourself: What possible good intentions could my spouse have regarding this behavior (even if I don't identify with the way he or she thinks)?

Accept and Allow Tactic #2: Don't Take It Personally!

When we don't practice accept and allow, our default reaction is to take our spouses' personality differences personally – as if they are purposely trying to annoy or frustrate us. This tendency is the source of a tremendous amount of blame, frustration, and anger in relationships.

Taylor brilliantly describes this struggle in her marriage:

TAYLOR: Franky is highly extroverted; I'm an introvert. My understanding of introversion and extroversion is that people who are introverted need time to recharge alone, whereas extroverts need time to recharge with people. Franky likes to have a nonstop, steady stream of people in his life, and he especially likes to have them over to the house. For me, the house is a sanctuary where I recharge. So now, after a lot of negotiating, he entertains on the first floor and doesn't obligate me to come down. I do my best to come down as much as I can, but sometimes I just need my space.

Also, every time Franky comes home, he opens the door and says, "Hello!" But not only that; when he says hello, he wants me to come running to greet him. Whereas when I come home, I kind of sneak in … I don't want to encounter anyone,

including him. I just want to put my stuff down and change my
energy... take my shoes off, maybe even change my clothes.
I just want time to myself because I've been out in the world.
That's just the way introverts are; sometimes we just need to
get away from everybody – even the people we love – because
we need the time to recharge.

It took many years for Franky to really understand how
much I need this recharge time. Maybe it's because, to an
extrovert, an introvert's desire for alone time feels like rejection.
And for an introvert, an extrovert's desire for constant company
feels like an intrusion. It's a very different psychology. But over
time, Franky has gradually accepted it. I think he used to take
it personally before, and now he realizes that it has nothing
to do with him. We're built differently, and he has different
needs. I also used to personalize it when we first got married.
I thought that his overwhelming need to talk and interact
with so many people was because of a defect in me, that he
found me boring. But when I realized that he's like this with
everyone – and I mean *everyone* – and that this is just the way
he is wired, I stopped taking it personally.

For years, Franky was taking Taylor's introversion personally.
Notice that when we take our spouses' behavior personally, what
we're saying is, "My spouse's behavior is about me." But if you
think about things logically, it's certainly more rational to think
that your spouse's behavior is more about him or her, and not
about you at all. It's always liberating to take ourselves out of the
center and realize that "it's not all about me!"

Exercise: Don't Take It Personally

To take the "personal sting" out of your spouse's behavior, try this exercise.

- To start, identify the specific behavior, personality trait, or characteristic of your spouse that you are taking personally. There may be more than one. Write them down.

- Ask yourself, "Is it possible that this is just the way my spouse is wired? That he or she just needs different things than I do? Is it possible that this tendency or behavior was not at all intended to upset me in any way?"

- It might also help to flip perspectives. Identify something about you (a behavior, a way of speaking, etc.) that your spouse might be personalizing, that has *nothing* to do with him or her. Reversing perspectives helps us regain the objectivity that our egos blur.

Accept and Allow Tactic #3: Let Go and Let It Be

Remember Vivian from chapter 5? Her husband Brett pursued her for two years in university and then continued, for one full year, through letters. In chapter 5, we saw how Brett utilized the tool of completion. For Vivian, the tactic of let go and let it be helped her take her marriage to the next level.

VIVIAN: A big difference between Brett and me is that I take time, in almost everything I do. He's fast; he does things quickly, sometimes impulsively. I plan. He can do many things at once, but I do things one at a time. He has this nonstop high energy that used to be a tremendous source of conflict. It was hard to live with someone who just couldn't sit still!

It's taken me a while, but I have realized that there are things in his personality that he cannot change. Now I realize that it is better for me to accept it; I try to just give him the freedom to be him. It helps me to do this, and many times I just forgive and forget.

Today, I appreciate his energy so much more. Brett definitely adds a lot of spunk to my life, and in general, his fast pace has moved us along in life. I've stopped complaining, and now it's so much easier to accept him as he is ... and I love him. We're married twenty-three years; we are so, so different ... sometimes it's comical how different we are. It's taken us a long time to build our marriage, but it's worth it all!

Vivian has not only come to accept Brett as he is, but she has taken a major step in realizing completion when she acknowledges that his fast pace is productive for their life as a couple.

Exercise: Let Go and Let It Be

Think of one particular trait or habit that annoys you in your spouse. Now reflect back to the info you gathered in the first two steps of the upward spiral:

- REFOCUS. Which innate resource(s) do you have in your marriage?
- COMPLETION. How does your spouse balance you out? Complement you as a team member?

Empowered by one or both of these answers, can you let go of something negative about your spouse that you were holding on to? Can you say to yourself, "I am accepting my spouse with this trait or habit – I am letting it be"? Can you "release" your spouse and give him or her permission to be?

Accept and Allow Tactic #4:
What Is My Spouse Putting Up with in Me?

When I asked Vivian about the temptation to change Brett, here's how our dialogue went:

CHANA: Vivian, did you ever try to change your husband?

VIVIAN: Oh, many times. A whole lot of my time went into changing him…

CHANA: How did that go? Did you get some good results?

VIVIAN: Nooo, absolutely not. Two years ago – after many years of futile efforts to change him – I realized I'd better change myself. Now, the things that used to bother me just don't bother me. I just told myself, "It's his character, that's it." The alternative – to focus on what I think he needs to change – is like asking for pain. You lose your peace of mind, your energy. Nothing good comes out of it. I've learned that it's better to be wise – to focus on your own stuff, to work on yourself instead of trying to change the person. And I have plenty of my own stuff. The more I remember this, the better our marriage is.

We are all a handful, but we so quickly forget that our spouses deal with our "stuff" as well. Vivian realized that focusing on her own folly was far more productive in her relationship than trying fruitlessly to change her husband. This attitude is a fantastic shortcut to stepping out of blame mode in a marriage. When we remember that our spouses are putting up with our flaws and inadequacies, we snap back into reality and suddenly find that we have much more energy and humility to accept them.

Exercise: What Is My Spouse Putting Up with in Me?

- On a daily basis, ask yourself, "What is my spouse putting up with in me?"
- Take a few minutes to think of two challenges that *you* bring to the relationship, two ways in which your partner has to put up with you. Write them down and remind yourself of them frequently.

Accept and Allow Tactic #5: Laugh It Up!

While attending a particular workshop (during my training as a couples therapist), I kept getting distracted by a couple sitting right in front of me. Although they looked like they were in their eighties, they also looked like they were on a honeymoon, not at a workshop. I was touched by the loving smiles they continually exchanged throughout the lecture and the way they kept looking out for one another, each making sure the other was OK.

When the lecturer called a fifteen-minute break, I turned to them and said, "The two of you are an adorable couple. I was sitting right behind you and couldn't help but notice how you kept checking in with each other. If you don't mind me asking, I was wondering how long you've been married?" The husband answered, "Not long enough!" After my long "aww," I asked, "Seriously, how long?" He said, "Guess!" I suggested fifty years and he replied, "Close! We are married fifty-six years!"

"What is the secret to your success?"

"You'll never believe us!"

"Try me!" I replied.

"Humor…we laugh our way through life. When we're dealing with annoying bureaucratic errands and everyone around us is complaining, we're cracking up. We laugh at ourselves, we laugh at our marriage. Since we argue a lot, we end up laughing at our marriage quite a bit."

Humor is one of the most important tools to help us to accept ourselves, our spouses, and our imperfect marriages. It's so helpful to learn how to laugh at ourselves and at our imperfect marriages (but not at our spouses!).

Exercise: Laugh It Up!

- Pick something that tends to frustrate you about yourself. Can you find something humorous in this tendency or habit? For example, you might be a bit OCD about everything having to be in a particular place. Or perhaps you are very indecisive. Can you see the humor in your tendency, just a bit? Now try to lighten up regarding a frustrating tendency or habit in your spouse.

- How can we bring humor into our marriages? I know one couple neither of whom is quick to laugh. They're both serious, sensitive, analytical thinkers. Since humor isn't in their emotional toolbox, it's hard for them to laugh off stress. So when they're going through a high-pressure phase of life, they plan comedy nights and stay up late watching old comedy shows. Once they start laughing, they relax, which in turn helps them to let go and see the humor in their own situation.

Accept and Allow Tactic #6: Step Out of Black-and-White Thinking

Randy, one of the men I interviewed, shared the following with me.

RANDY: My wife Alexis and I are a great match, except in one area – she thinks I'm too touchy-feely. Make no mistake about it – she is a warm, caring person. But she's not all that expressive with physical affection. I always considered myself to be the normal one. When I spend time with Alexis's family, it's pretty obvious to me that they're very reserved. Compared to my family, I'd even say that they're a bit cold.

It took me a long time to come to terms with her nature. It's really frustrating when you just want to hug your wife, and she "needs her space." I definitely spent a few years judging her and her family, which definitely didn't take me or us to a good place. I was pretty stuck until a colleague of mine told me that he had a similar dynamic with his wife. But he was pretty chilled about the whole thing…he just took it in stride.

I realized that part of my block was that I had decided that touchy-feely was normal and good; in my mind, loving couples behaved this way. When I started to consider the possibility that people who need more physical space might *also* be normal – and just as loving, in a different way – I started to chill out as well.

Black-and-white thinking is very judgmental and limiting. It dismisses a range or spectrum of possibilities and instead puts people into simplistic categories of right or wrong, good or bad, normal or abnormal. Fact is, there are as many styles of relationships as there are couples. Each couple is a unique organism. Only when we stop thinking in black-and-white terms are we able to discover the unique individuality of each couple.

When Randy discovered that there actually could be other types of "normal," he opened his eyes to new possibilities. He shared his new insights:

RANDY: Now I realize that I did this with all of my girlfriends. I decided that they were "not normal" because they also needed more space than I did. It's funny, it seems that I'm only attracted to women who need more space! But slowly, slowly, I'm learning how to hold back some of what they would call excess physical affection, and I'm starting to feel close to Alexis in other ways, besides touch.

And you know, once I began doing this, I realized that Alexis does all these things to express her love that I never really appreciated before – little things, like setting up my coffee in the morning and buying books she thinks I'll like. The more I take in these little acts of love, the less I feel the intense need for physical affection.

When we're stuck in black and white, we bulldoze over the nuances and intricacies hidden within every human behavior. Do you have any traits, behaviors, etc., that you think are normal, but seem to be judged by others as wrong or abnormal? How does this feel? What are some of the aspects of this trait or behavior you wish others could appreciate?

Exercise: Step Out of Black-and-White Thinking

- Pick one behavior that you have been judgmental about in your spouse (I'm not referring to objectively extreme behaviors, such as addictions and compulsions). Have you been judging this behavior in a black-and-white way (wrong, bad, abnormal)? What are the possible other sides/nuances/interesting aspects of this behavior that you might have been glossing over until now? What are possible reasons it could be normal – just a different normal from your own way?

- Imagine that you are in court working as a highly paid defense attorney, defending your spouse's behavior or personality trait. What positive arguments could you make in his or her defense?

Accept and Allow Tactic #7: Take Joy in Your Spouse's Joy

When we fight against the way people are, we resist their very being. When we are at peace with the truth of how people are, however, we accept and allow them to be themselves, and we can enjoy seeing them in their element, doing their thing – even if we cannot relate to it or it's something that originally or instinctively annoys us. This is what happened with Franky (the super-extrovert) and Taylor (the introvert who needed serious "recharge time"), after they practiced accept and allow.

TAYLOR: With time, I've been able to step out of my shell more often. As a result, these days we both enjoy hosting couples in our home for educational workshops. I think that when Franky stopped trying to change me, I discovered that hosting these workshops stretches my introversion – in a healthy way. And during these gatherings, I really enjoy watching Franky work the crowd. He's so great at it, and I'm proud to be by his side.

Taylor also shared another incident that had happened.

TAYLOR: A while ago, Franky did the cutest thing. I was sitting there reading a book in my typical introverted style and he said, "I see that you're really enjoying that book over there. Can I bring you a coffee to sip on, while you read?" It was an awesome moment, because in the past, he would have been sort of jealous of my book. This time, I felt like he really appreciated my reading time. It made me feel really close to him.

Both Taylor and Franky show us that when we view our spouses' personality differences in an accepting way, we can come to truly enjoy the very thing that irritated us.

Exercise: Take Joy in Your Spouse's Joy

When our spouses are involved in something that we don't like to do (or can't relate to), we tend to feel excluded and/or distanced. But when we simply take joy in the fact that they're happy – and feel their joy – this can automatically help us feel included.

- It helps to ask yourself, "How does the fact that my spouse has this tendency enrich my team?" Remember, if it enriches your spouse, it automatically enriches your team.

- Take a few moments to watch your spouse doing his or her thing, in a state of "engaged flow." If you can say (and eventually feel), "Wow, I'm so happy that you're happy now," you might actually "catch" some of your spouse's happiness. At the very least, you will make his or her day.

- Is there something you can buy or make for your spouse that would enhance his or her experience of your unshared behavior or personality trait? For example, if your spouse likes to spend large amounts of time fixing things, could you buy a new tool? Or find an article that discusses a new gadget? Or, if your spouse is into organization, could you find an item or article that might be helpful toward furthering this personality trait?

How to Lose Two Hundred Pounds

The more we can accept our spouses for who they are and assume that their behavior is just a part of their personalities, the more we can step out of judgment, let go, and "allow" them to be themselves. This letting go feels like a release of two hundred extra pounds, because when we are not in a mode of acceptance, so much of our precious energy goes into resisting our spouses. Accept and allow is not a passive state; it is an active process that leads to freedom and peace, respect and love – and opens the gate for renewed attraction. When we release the extra emotional weight (which inhibits any forward motion in a relationship), we find ourselves wondering, "What took me so long?"

> "The more we can accept our spouses for who they are, the more we can step out of judgment, let go, and "allow" them to be themselves."

The great news is that the upward spiral keeps ascending, if you continue utilizing the tools in this book. Once you experience accept and allow, you can refocus better. Which *then* leads you to see the completion between you and your spouse in a more profound way. Which *then* leads to a higher level of accept and allow. And so on and so forth. The upward spiral just keeps going. And the higher you go, the broader the view and perspective you have of the beauty and profundity of your unique marriage. As a result, your marriage becomes a dynamic, alive, vibrant entity – a loving relationship.

Transforming Your Relationship

Chapter 9

A Case Study Illustrating the Upward Spiral

You met Helene and Eric in chapter 3; they are the introverted-extroverted couple who had their rude awakening in the Rockies, tried to change each other, and traveled the downward spiral until they were both miserable. This chapter will map out how they succeeded in learning to live – and love – with their differences by traveling the upward spiral.

Step One: Refocus – Accessing Resources

The first step for Helene and Eric was to access their innate resources. Eric was immediately inspired by a virtue in Helene – her serenity. He was captivated by her calm nature from the moment he met her; it absolutely intrigued him. Helene appreciated a strong value she shared with Eric: integrity. She first met him at work and was continually impressed by his honesty and commitment to follow through, no matter what. This was a value they shared –

and, incidentally, a shared personality trait that stemmed from their shared value.

Other resources they shared included a similar value (the same religion) plus one lifestyle similarity (a mutual love of the outdoors). Remembering these resources helped Helene and Eric feel more connected, just a bit. However, it was shortlived because they only intellectualized this information and were not yet able to bring it to life.

Step Two: Tap into Completion – The Completion Switches

In chapters 5 and 6 we introduced nine completion switches to help couples turn on the lights in their marriages to effectively tap into completion. What does using these switches look like in action? Let's take the example of Helene and Eric to see how this can work in a real-life situation.

Over time, Helene had become more and more reactive to Eric's "over-friendliness" to everyone around him; he seemed to be more eager to connect to mere strangers than to sit and talk with her. And when they were actually sitting and talking, he would often answer his phone, saying that this was a very important call. At times, Helene's annoyance grew to outrage.

As for Eric, he was feeling more and more claustrophobic around Helene. He was putting a ton of effort into spending quality time with her and giving her what he considered his "undivided attention." Despite his effort, Eric felt he wasn't getting anywhere. The harder he tried, the more defeated he felt.

The more Eric and Helene focused on what the other was doing wrong, the more annoyed they both became. As a result, they reinforced and fortified their personality differences, and the gap between them grew wider. When I met them, Helene was in a very bad place; she felt, in her words, too "emotionally drained" to work on the relationship. So, initially I worked only with Eric. In addition to remembering the resources he shared with Helene (outlined above), he started to flip the completion switches.

COMPLETION SWITCH #1: LOOKING INWARD. Eric asked himself, "In order to improve my marriage, what do I need to work on?" He thought back to his ex-girlfriends; they all felt that he was too "out there" with other people and not inner-focused or relationship-focused enough. He realized that this pattern was something he needed to work on, to be a more balanced person.

COMPLETION SWITCH #2: THE INITIAL ATTRACTION. Eric was initially attracted to Helene's introverted side! However, on a conscious level, he didn't think of her quality as "introversion"; he just felt very grounded and centered around her and wasn't quite sure why. After marriage, when he opened his eyes to her introverted nature, and it began to challenge him, he felt more distanced from Helene. Using the completion mindset, he was able to reframe her introversion in a positive light and thus reconnect to the strong initial attraction he had felt toward her when they were dating.

COMPLETION SWITCH #3: FREEDOM FROM YOUR COMFORT ZONE. Eric's comfort zone was social settings – working a room full of people. Having an intimate conversation was not his typical idea of a good time. He didn't want to lose his personality in the process, so he took small, steady steps toward change. His first step was a commitment to spend dinner time with Helene – completely focused on her, no phone calls, no computer checking. Although Eric initially felt some discomfort, he pushed through and began to feel that inner joy that surfaces when we're growing.

COMPLETION SWITCH #4: THE CURIOSITY CURE. In this stage, Eric discovered an additional perk of being married to an opposite:

there is always something new to explore about your spouse and his or her perspective on life. Also, he remembered being bored in his previous relationships and began to be open to the idea that he and Helene – because of their differences – could have a more dynamic relationship, which he craved. Eric began to ask Helene questions about herself and her thought process, something he hadn't done in quite a while. Helene felt more "seen" by Eric; Eric felt more authentically interested in his wife.

COMPLETION SWITCH #6: REJOICING IN THE GIFT. Eric was initially drawn to Helene because she centered him; she helped him to connect to his "wise self," as he put it. This was the gift Eric saw in her. He used to revel in this newfound part of himself, which he got in touch with when he first started dating her. As Eric shifted his focus from the challenge that accompanies introversion to the gift that comes with this trait, he felt a whole lot lighter.

COMPLETION SWITCH #8: CELEBRATING YOUR TEAM VICTORIES. In a later session, Eric began to focus on their potential team power. When he thought about his growing kids, he realized that Helene's internal side was a quality he considered of extreme importance in parenting. Eric realized that if his wife were half as outgoing as he was, their children might miss out on the kind of well-rounded upbringing he thought his kids would need. As Eric reviewed all of the ways Helene contributed to the greater whole of their marriage, he realized something: when he had been so caught up in their personality differences, he completely forgot that they were a team at all. He now started to appreciate – and celebrate – the victories that their personality differences afforded their children.

I worked with Eric (separately) for three months. Since he and Helene shared a love of the outdoors, I suggested that he take Helene out for a couple of picnics or hikes. Throughout the three months, Helene saw that Eric was really trying to be more present with her and felt a lot of positive energy coming from him.

As Helene began to warm up to Eric again, she also started to focus on her own growth (rather than trying to change Eric). In particular, she started to own her anger and to face her tendency to snap whenever he would annoy her. She also tried to focus on the gift of Eric's outgoing side, instead of the challenges it presented. As a result, her feelings toward Eric took a sharp turn for the better. Eric was amazed by the effect that his unilateral changes had on his wife.

Research underscores the importance of personality differences in helping a marriage thrive. According to Dr. Robert Levenson of the University of California, Berkeley, studies found that personality *similarities* were associated with decreased marital satisfaction over a twelve-year period. According to Levenson, "This may be because, over the long haul, different personalities may provide couples with complementary resources for dealing with life's challenges."*

Completion is a powerful tool that keeps the light shining brightly in a marriage. This bright light can even illuminate the next generation. Before my daughter got married, she said to me, "Mom, I'm so glad that you're disorganized." I thought she was joking around, but she was totally serious. She then explained herself: "Mom, you know that I'm really organized, sometimes to a fault. Sometimes I wonder to myself, what would have happened if I had a super organized mother? I would be so wound up today. Thank G-d, you're so chilled, laid-back... and disorganized. Over

---

* Robert W. Levenson and Michelle N Shiota, "Birds of a Feather Don't Always Fly Farthest: Similarity in Big Five Personality Predicts More Negative Marital Satisfaction Trajectories in Long-Term Marriages," *Psychology and Aging* 22, no. 4 (2007): 666–75.

the years, you totally chilled me out and prepared me to deal with other disorganized people in my life."

Well, I'm glad that my disorganization counted for something! Not to be defensive or anything, but I have become much more organized over the years. And yet, to my dismay, truly organized people – people who are born that way – can see that I'm still "in process." I'll keep stretching, it's great. It helps me to be more balanced. But it's always nice to see that even our challenges can impact our families in a positive way when seen through the lens of completion.

Step Three: Accept and Allow – The Seven Tools

We saw above how Helene and Eric were able to tap into completion to get the most out of the powerful harmony in their personality differences. This enabled them to go beyond some of the opposition they had to their conflicting traits – but there still was some work to do. This is where the seven tools of accept and allow came into the picture.

1. SEARCH FOR GOOD INTENT. When Eric searched for positive intent in his wife, he was in for a surprise. He hadn't realized the degree to which he was interpreting Helene's behavior as a nagging attempt to bother him. Focusing on Helene's good intentions allowed him to see that she sincerely desired a close relationship. This helped him understand Helene's need for intimate one-on-one connection much better, especially since she came from a close-knit family of people with a high regard for family privacy. For the first time, he could see her need for intimate time with him as a positive thing. This realization renewed and revitalized his attraction to Helene.

2. DON'T TAKE IT PERSONALLY! Helene was surprised to discover that deep down inside, she often thought Eric was trying to upset

her when he talked to other people in her presence. When she took the focus off of herself, she recognized that this is just the way Eric is. Even when he was two years old, he was the center of attention and always loved being around people. The more she understood this, the less apt she was to take his behavior personally.

3. LET GO AND LET IT BE. Helene used the technique of refocus to remind herself of her absolute love of Eric's honesty and integrity, which she had found so attractive when they dated. In addition, she acknowledged the completion in their relationship by remembering how his playfulness and fun/outgoing side really pulled her out of her shell back then. Both of these steps, combined with her new ability not to personalize his behavior, enabled her to let go and let him do his thing more, when they were in public settings. This in turn helped her to reconnect to the strong initial attraction she had to Eric.

4. WHAT IS MY SPOUSE PUTTING UP WITH IN ME? Eric was very humbled when he realized that it wasn't always a picnic to live with his hyper-hectic energy and his tendency to slack off regarding his responsibilities. As a result, he was able to accept Helene without having to try as hard.

5. LAUGH IT UP! To stop getting so annoyed by Helene, Eric (who has a fantastic sense of humor) decided to make up a funny word to say to himself. He came up with a crazy word ("blurf") and would crack himself up at times. After a while, Helene caught on, and this funny word became *their* code word – they would say it whenever they started getting judgmental about their differences. It was their way to remind themselves to lighten up, let go, and laugh at themselves.

6. STEP OUT OF BLACK-AND-WHITE THINKING. Helene was stuck in the black-and-white thinking of "If my spouse loves me,

he will give me his undivided attention." After all, this was the way her parents interacted; it was her only model of how a "normal" couple should be. Then she started to open her mind up to the possibility of a different style of relationship. She saw how some great couples enjoyed quite a bit of space in their relationship; this was also "normal." Understanding this freed up Helene – and Eric – to explore and further develop their very own style of relationship, based on their unique combination of personality differences and personal histories.

7. TAKE JOY IN YOUR SPOUSE'S JOY. As Helene's acceptance of Eric grew, she was able to release him and let him get out there to work the crowd. Helene even started to enjoy watching him do his thing. She was even more surprised (and sometimes shocked) to find Eric – of his own volition – seeking out times for their more intimate one-on-one talks. Likewise, with time, Eric was increasingly motivated by the joy he felt as a result of seeing her so happy when he initiated time together as a couple – without Helene asking for it. Eric started to consider himself lucky to be married to someone so good at building close relationships. He too was surprised to see that as he initiated more intimate time together, she in turn gave him more space to get out there and do his thing.

What came first, the chicken or the egg? Did Helene's release on Eric start the ball rolling, or did Eric's release on Helene create the change? It doesn't matter who started it. Even if only Helene or Eric were to unilaterally accept and allow, there would have been a positive change in the relationship.

What Can It Do for You?

We've seen that working the upward spiral brought about a beautiful transformation in Eric and Helene's marriage. In step one, refocus, they identified and accessed their resources. In step two, they tapped into completion by flipping the various completion switches to discover both personal harmony and teamwork/synergy. Finally, in the third step they practiced the seven tools of accept and allow to truly live the freedom of allowing each other to be themselves. And as we saw, they did not both have to be on board to start the process of climbing the upward spiral: Eric started by himself, and his efforts brought enough light to the marriage to launch the two of them firmly up the upward spiral and into a whole new phase of their marriage.

What can the upward spiral do for you?

Chapter 10

A Loving Relationship

Often, people ask me, "Why is respect so important in a relationship?" When I explain that respect is the foundation of love – that it's actually the prerequisite of real love – I tend to get a puzzled look. That's when I explain the connection between the three-step upward spiral (refocus, tap into completion, and accept and allow) and respect and love.

What is respect? It is a positive feeling of admiration for a person. One major challenge in any close relationship, and especially in marriage (when we live with a person day in and day out), is that the more you know someone, the more acquainted you become with that person's faults. As a result, the "admiration" often wears off. This is why respect often goes out the window in marriage.

The solution to this dilemma is actually hidden within the word *respect*:

re- = "once more," as in <u>re</u>new, <u>re</u>fresh, <u>re</u>cycle
-spect = "to see," as in in<u>spect</u>, su<u>spect</u>, intro<u>spect</u>

Therefore, the way to generate respect is to consciously "see again" – in our case, to take a second look at the profundity of your complementary differences and different ways of thinking.

To see that two plus two equals four, but so does three plus one... and that's great. Respect teaches us that the other person is not us – neither an extension of us nor a reflection of us. Respect enables us to see others as unique individuals and appreciate their unique differences.

The three-step upward spiral process of refocus, tap into completion, and accept and allow opens our eyes to see again and again, which rekindles admiration:

- Refocus: To see and access the innate resources already in our relationship.
- Tap into completion: To see the underlying wisdom behind our initial attraction.
- Accept and allow: To get rid of the judgment and negativity that blind us from continuing to see the way we complete each other. The degree to which we can accept our spouses with their differences and see them for who they are is the degree to which we can truly respect them.

Let's take a look at how this works in action. When Michelle came to speak with me about her troubled marriage, I asked if she respected her husband, Brendon. She started laughing. All she could see in Brendon was his "flaw": he was too "chilled out." "Why can't he just buckle down and get a solid job like I have? He keeps dabbling with this flimsy real estate business that he inherited from his friend." Michelle was heading down the downward spiral – fast.

I asked Michelle, "Why did you marry Brendon? What initially drew you to him?" Michelle was clear: "He was fun, playful, and easygoing. Our energies worked so well together. He really chilled me out. I definitely had my concerns about his job status, but I had dated a lot of top earners. Something was always missing in our connection. But Brendon and I had great chemistry, and he really brought out the best in me."

Although Michelle remembered this – and actually had identified the completion that Brendon's personality brought to her in their marriage – that alone didn't help. At this point, her knowledge wasn't internalized; it was just an intellectual awareness. She kept saying, "How can I respect him? He's sitting around, wasting his time!"

This is how the rest of our session went:

CHANA: I hear you, Michelle. Let's go back to your dating days. Was he very busy and proactive back then?

MICHELLE: No... not really. But it didn't bother me then. I was just having a really good time with him. I guess I didn't care back then because I was focused on the good.

CHANA: Uh-huh. And now?

MICHELLE: Now it *really* bothers me. It's really hard. I'm such an over achiever; compared to me, Brendon is lazy. And financially, we're not doing great. My best friend keeps telling me that I knew what I was getting myself into. I did. Sort of. I mean, I didn't realize how hard it would be. In my better moments, I remember the good things, what I love about him. I remember that he is the only man I ever really wanted to marry. But those better moments are becoming more rare. I wish they weren't... which is why I came to see you.

Michelle and I jumped right into the three-step approach:

1. REFOCUS. Michelle took time to appreciate the innate resources she had in her marriage. She wrote them down and reviewed them every day.

2. TAP INTO COMPLETION. Michelle admitted that she is very moody at times and has a tendency to get really angry. Brendon's calm, laid-back demeanor helped balance her out. She had fallen into the trap of focusing on the negative side of

Brendon's mellowness and forgetting about the positive. I gave her exercises to focus daily on Brendon's gifts. (Specifically, we focused on completion switch #5, swapping shoes; refer to chapter 5.)

3. ACCEPT AND ALLOW. First off, Michelle started to focus on what Brendon was putting up with in her (accept and allow tactic #3; see chapter 8). She finally got it; her anger *was* a big deal. Until now, she had conveniently overlooked this fact. When she focused on this truth, she was humbled and started to really appreciate what Brendon was putting up with and accepting, in her. This helped her to accept Brendon more and more.

Still, Michelle did struggle with the fact that her husband might never be a major breadwinner. She wrestled with this fact for quite a while until she had an epiphany of sorts. Michelle realized that on some semi-conscious level (before marriage), she had known that she would have to be the breadwinner in their relationship. Money was *not* the reason she had married him; his "chilled-out" personality and the way he balanced her out *was* the reason.

Like a domino effect, the more Michelle accepted Brendon, the more she freed him up to be . . . Brendon. As Michelle connected to all the things she loved about her husband, she found the strength and integrity to embrace the truth about his "earning power" and make it work for their marriage.

By changing how she thought, Michelle changed how she felt about her husband. That's because behind every single feeling is a thought. If you can change how you think (by applying the three-step process), you can change how you feel. In other words, when Michelle thought about Brendon differently, she could *re-see* him in a different light. As a result, her admiration was reignited, and it suddenly became so much easier to respect her husband.

Your Spouse Is an Artist

You can also think of re-seeing this way: Someone who respects a certain painter won't just glance at the artist's work – he'll examine every brushstroke and dash of color again and again, trying to see how it all harmonizes together. But if this person buys the painting and sees it day in and day out, what will happen to some of that amazement? Even here, some of it will wear off. That person will now have to consciously "re-see" those brushstrokes – so as to regenerate that admiration. When couples stop re-seeing each other, when they no longer appreciate their partners' individual brushstrokes, disrespect seeps into the marriage.

I want to share a conversation I had with Andy, a very articulate and well thought-out man. He was twenty-two years into his marriage at the time of our interview. "I've finally figured out how to respect my wife," he told me, "but there definitely were some major bumps along the road."

ANDY: At the beginning of our marriage, I was very frustrated – really exasperated. Laura's need for reassurance was a major source of tension because she tends to crave a lot more safety than I do. Even after twenty-two years of marriage, whenever I have to deal with someone on our behalf, she needs to know what I'm going to say or do. For me, it's "Don't worry, I'll handle it." But Laura says, "No, you have to tell me what you're going to say or do; rehearse with me."

For years, I looked at this tendency like a chronic illness; it would show up in so many different ways. I definitely lost a lot of respect for Laura, because of it. But today, my response to her behavior is acceptance. I say to myself, "We're all put together differently," and I recognize that my wife needs a lot more safety than I do.

How did Andy arrive at this place of wholehearted acceptance of Laura? He spoke to me about his accept and allow process: "Look, Laura is an amazing human being," Andy began. "When I met her, the first thing that touched me was how loyal she was to her friends and even to her family who weren't necessarily that good to her. I really love this quality in her and have tried to develop it in myself. She is so genuine, so real...so good-hearted." Andy was a master at refocus; he clearly remembered Laura's virtues. By reminding himself of these things over the years, he innately tapped into the power of refocus.

Next, Andy shared with me how well Laura balances him out – the completion in their relationship.

ANDY: She definitely grounds me a lot. I'm all over the place, a big extrovert, and sometimes speak without thinking. My filter needs some work. Laura always says, "If you have tact, you don't have to retract." I can put my foot in my mouth and have had to go back and apologize or explain myself. This *never* happens to her. I'd like to think I've gotten better...that my filter is slowly developing.

Over the years, I've grown. I've developed more compassion and patience. I recognize my weaknesses – and my wife's strengths. I guess all of this has helped me to get to a place where I appreciate her so much today.

Andy really got it. Because he paid attention to Laura's brush-strokes, he taught himself to stay connected to Laura's gifts and what drew him to her in the first place. And as he gained *appreciation* for these traits, not only did he start to develop them in himself, but his respect for Laura was boosted.

Interestingly, there are two ways of defining the word *appreciation*:

- To recognize something's or someone's worth.
- To go up in price, e.g., the appreciation of real estate or jewelry. When something goes up in price, it appreciates.

These two definitions are connected: When you appreciate something, it becomes more valuable. And if you appreciate your marriage, your marriage will appreciate.

"If you appreciate your marriage, your marriage will appreciate."

Respect Begets Respect; Disrespect Begets Disrespect

People are often surprised to hear that we can "will" feelings of respect for another person. Danielle was one of them. She grew up watching her mother disrespect her father – the disrespect was almost tangible in the house. Her mother's mantra was, "When your father acts in a way that deserves respect, I'll give it to him. He has to earn it first." As a child, Danielle was so disgusted by the way her mother disrespected her father. She promised herself that she wouldn't make this mistake in her own marriage.

When Danielle started dating, she purposely looked for a husband whom she could look up to and respect. When she met Joey, she was attracted to his brilliance, honesty, and diligence. Soon after the wedding, however, she found herself focusing on his weaknesses instead of his strengths.

"I knew that my husband wasn't the social type of guy," Danielle told me. "But once we got married, all I saw was his social awkwardness. It's almost as if I couldn't see the other wonderful traits I knew were there." Every time they went out with friends or to an office party, Danielle became increasingly embarrassed by her husband's public persona. Disrespect quickly followed.

Eventually, they had only one piece left of their marriage: their shared parenting tasks. Otherwise, they were living parallel lives.

In my first session with Danielle, I explained the downward spiral to her; she clearly saw this in her own marriage – and in her parents' relationship. And she really wanted a change. So we came up with a plan of action for the next few months:

- REFOCUS. Every day, Danielle would spend time refocusing on Joey's outstanding virtues – his brilliance, honesty, and diligence. And she would make sure to comment to Joey regarding her appreciation of these gifts.
- TAP INTO COMPLETION. Danielle would write down and focus on her own flaws and look for ways to better herself (completion switch #1, looking inward; see chapter 5), instead of focusing on Joey's. Once she had some of this step down, we moved to completion switch #7, dividing and conquering (see chapter 6): she would focus on the team power they had, due to their complementary differences.
- ACCEPT AND ALLOW. Simultaneously, she would remind herself that Joey was putting up with and accepting her stuff, rather than throwing it in her face (accept and allow tactic #3; see chapter 8).

It took a lot of effort for Danielle to break her habit of focusing on her husband's flaws, but she kept at it. With time, her admiration for Joey shot up. Respect started to flow, and Joey reciprocated immediately by showing her more respect. In a matter of months, I watched their marriage turn around. Respect begets respect; disrespect begets disrespect.

Creating Respect

Although the three-step process generates authentic respect that comes from within oneself, it is also helpful to adapt external respect-generating behaviors, such as:

- Learn to compliment. Your *sincere* complimentary remarks about your partner's mental abilities, physical traits, financial wisdom, spiritual growth, or any other noteworthy attribute can go a long way.
- Demonstrate that you feel your partner is important by sincerely taking interest in what he or she thinks is important.
- Acknowledge and appreciate your partner's successes.
- Stand by your partner when others treat him or her disrespectfully.
- Follow through on what your partner asks you to do.
- Be respectful with your body language (e.g., smile).
- Make quality time for your partner.
- Ask for your partner's advice.
- Listen attentively without interrupting.
- Express gratitude at every opportunity...and mean it.

Back at the beginning of this chapter, I mentioned that respect is a prerequisite for love. This is the deal: we can respect people without loving them – but love without respect will not last or be healthy. That's why – especially in marriage – respect has to precede love. Even between parent and child, lack of respect interferes with love; if respect is absent, parents can "love" their children and be so attached that they cannot let go. These parents are unable to *see* their children's real needs, wishes, opinions, and ideas.

Take for example, a parent who arrives home and sees his or her child deeply engrossed in play. This parent, excited to see the child, picks the kid up to give him or her a hug. But the child is squirming after having been ripped away from a moment of play. Who was that hug for? Certainly not for the child. This is what love looks like, without respect. Without a basis of respect, love can become self-absorbed and selfish.

As we've seen throughout this chapter, respect demands that we "re-see" and accept – not try to change or control – people. Love without respect can crush the other person. Respect teaches us that the other person is not an extension or a reflection of us. Respect makes it possible for us to *see* others as unique individuals and appreciate their unique differences. Once this is in place, we are ready to love. I like to compare love to a flower that can only grow and blossom in soil that is rich in respect and appreciation.

Cultivating Love

We've learned how to cultivate respect. How do we cultivate love? In my first book, *I Only Want to Get Married Once*, I discuss the fact that love is not just a feeling; it is also a verb. I explain there that the feeling of love is continuously generated when we feed it with specific actions. The most important of these actions is giving.

But does giving always lead to love? Every couples therapist can think of situations in which partners felt that they gave so much, with little or no results. One couple that comes to mind from my own practice is Anna and Guy.

When I first met this couple, they were young, struggling newlyweds. Growing up, Guy was convinced that he was going to be the perfect husband. He watched his father lovingly serve breakfast in bed to his mother on various occasions and decided that this was something he would surely do as a good husband. In our session, Guy complained to me, "I don't understand... I'm such a good husband. She doesn't appreciate anything I do. I even make her breakfast in bed!" Anna rolled her eyes and retorted, "I told you so many times, *I don't eat breakfast!*" This is a great example of what I call *non*-custom-made giving. Guy wanted to give without checking what his wife actually wanted.

If we don't direct our giving specifically to our spouses' needs, the effects might not be so positive. There is a great story about a little boy who came home all bruised, with his clothes torn. His mother was shocked: "What in the world happened?" The boy responded, "I was helping an old lady cross the street." His mother asked, "So why do you look like that?" His reply: "Because she didn't want to go!"

There are two major challenges of giving:

- We tend to overemphasize what we're giving and minimize what our spouses are giving.
- We tend to project our needs onto others and give them what we would want, rather than what they need or want.

Although "generic giving" such as making dinner for your spouse or bringing home a gift is a wonderful way to generate love, there is a much deeper and more powerful level of giving. This is what I call "customized giving": it's the type of giving we can only do when we respect our partners' personality differences and therefore see what they really need.

Justin and Gail exemplify incredible custom-made giving. Justin explained:

JUSTIN: Gail has a hard time with decisions . . . not just what she should do at work or for her family, but even what to eat. She often defers to me and asks for my help. I used to get really impatient; it was annoying. I'd think to myself, "How many times have we come to the same restaurant?"

Today I'm less annoyed. I understand that it's something

she needs. Although I do gently encourage her to make her own decisions, I've accepted that for now, this is one of my roles in our marriage. Instead of trying to turn her into a decisive person, I've come to understand that for whatever reason, decisions are actually painful for her. As a result, I'm learning that I can give to her in two opposite ways: there are times when she needs me to encourage her to make decisions and there are other times when she authentically needs my input.

Custom-made giving feeds marriages, in the most profound way. This is what Justin teaches us; he learned to give according to Gail's personality needs, not according to his own personality needs.

When I asked Justin whether there were any benefits to being married to a less decisive partner, he replied:

JUSTIN: It's funny, I wouldn't have said this a while ago, but today, I definitely think that there are benefits that I never considered. The main one is that we're always interacting. And when I ask her to narrow a choice down, it helps me to understand who she is. I find people to be fascinating. Plus, it stretches me and helps me strengthen my decisive muscles. It's pushed me to micromanage my thoughts and feelings. It's helped me to grow. I always tell my friends that marriage is the ultimate opportunity for personal growth and exploration of humankind; it's such a powerful experience.

Gail likewise sees the tremendous value of their personality differences:

GAIL: In general, I am better with people than Justin is. He is more introverted and is better one-on-one. In social settings, he prefers that the attention is on me – so I play the social side of our marriage. He really appreciates this. But I will add that he has gotten a lot better in group settings, since we've been married. I think I rubbed off on him a bit.

Every time Gail steps into a conversation to save Justin from feeling uncomfortable, she is *custom-giving* to him. Every time Justin helps Gail with her decisions, he is *custom-giving* Gail the gift of, as she puts it, "security, comfort, and relief." Only when we accept our spouses' differences can we begin to really see what they truly need – and fine-tune our giving as a result. Really, it's *because* of our personality differences that we each have something unique to give to our marriage and to our children.

Avoid Negative Giving

An important caveat: besides undirected giving, there are other types of giving that do not generate love. I call these types "negative giving," because they have detrimental effects. You'll notice that these types of giving lack the foundation of respect we discussed above:

- Giving without boundaries, which could create dependency, depletion of self, loss of self, etc.
- Giving in order to get – or so that your spouse owes you.
- Giving with strings attached.
- Giving as an escape from oneself.
- Giving in order to demonstrate how much more *you* give to the relationship.

These types of giving don't leave the giver or the receiver changed for the better. Negative giving can harm us rather than build us.

Loving You Is Building Me

I often tell my clients the story of the elderly carpenter who spent his life building homes. He informed his boss about his plans to retire from the house-building industry; the time had come to relax and spend quality time with his wife and extended family. His boss was sad to let such a great worker go and requested that he build just one more house (as a personal favor). The carpenter was annoyed but agreed. His ambivalence led him to do a sloppy job while using the cheapest materials.

The boss came to check the house out when it was completed. As he handed the house keys over to the retiring carpenter, the boss said, "This is your house – it's my retirement gift to you." You can imagine the shock of the carpenter. The first thought that crossed his mind was, "If only I had known…"

The same lesson applies to couples: every single day, we are building our marriages. We're a team, so if we cheat our spouses, we cheat ourselves. If we disrespect our spouses, we disrespect ourselves (and our marriages). When we give to our spouses, we are giving to ourselves.

The bigger question is, "Can I even see what my spouse is giving to me?" And then, "Am I taking in the things that my spouse gives me?" And then, "Am I expressing my gratitude?" One of our biggest problems is that we take so much for granted – especially from those closest to us. It's essential to spend a few moments every day asking ourselves, "What is my spouse doing for me?" Examine even the most mundane things. Do we *see* and take in what our spouses are doing for us – especially the things that we don't like to do, want to do, or know how to do?* Once we examine

---

* In Hebrew, the word for gratitude is *hakarat hatov*, which literally means "recognizing (or seeing) the good."

and see these things, it's essential to grab the moment and say a sincere "thank you"! Gratitude is powerful; it's a real relationship changer and booster.

Recharging Your Marriage

One of my favorite sayings is "A great marriage doesn't happen when the perfect couple gets together; it happens when an imperfect couple gets together to enjoy each other's differences." This is so true, and now we have the tools to really put this into practice. On a conscious level, the initial attraction to a spouse is based on a physical, intellectual, emotional, and/or spiritual connection. To create this bond, people actively look for similarities. But, subconsciously, a driving force behind the initial spark is often personality *differences*. That's because, as we have explained throughout this book, the adhesion of a couple comes from an unconscious magnetism between two opposites. Once we know how to tap into the benefits of our personality differences, they can act as a *battery* to continuously reenergize that connection. And that's when it hits us: "Oh – *that's* why I married you!" It is then that we can not only live with our personality differences... but *love* with our differences.

Carl, one of the men in my relationship study, expressed it this way:

CARL: The beautiful thing about opposites is that there is always something new to explore about the person. There's always more to discover about each other. That's why marriage is such an incredible journey – you never stop learning.

On a personal level, I'll never forget, when I was dating my husband, one of the things that blew me away about him was his brain. He was (and still is) like a walking encyclopedia; he could discuss anything from physics to cooking, on a very high level. I remember thinking to myself one night, after a great date, "Wow...my brain hurts!" I realized that just by being around my husband, I was stretching my mind. As a creative, artsy type of person, I guess I had let my analytical mind get pretty rusty.

But today, twenty-seven years later, even though I don't pick up physics books for fun, my analytical thought process is much more developed. As a matter of fact, the writing of this book was certainly enhanced by the influence my marriage has had on me. Therefore, if there is something in this book that doesn't make sense, you can blame my husband. But seriously, as the years of our marriage pass, I am more and more appreciative of the power of completion, and who we have become, because of each other.

Today, people question the validity of a lifelong marriage. They don't realize that it takes exactly a *lifetime* to build a healthy marriage and reap the benefits. The key to success is to visualize your marriage as a *vehicle* to take you through life – in partnership. At different moments in the marriage, one is the leader, the other is the follower. Each spouse is a teacher. Each is a learner.

When we understand that marriage is not based on thinking alike, we can finally start to think together. Then, marriage becomes a journey to a rich, expansive, and profound life together. Bon voyage!

"When we understand that marriage is not based on thinking alike, we can finally start to think together."

Chapter 11

Tips for All Ten Personality Differences

This is not intended to be a comprehensive list or code for all types of personality differences. It is simply a list of the ten most common personality differences that surfaced in my research:

1. Spender/saver
2. Extrovert/introvert
3. Organized/not-so-organized
4. Emotional/intellectual
5. Faster paced/slower paced
6. More affectionate/less affectionate
7. Optimist/pessimist
8. Doer/"be-er"
9. Very giving/more restrained
10. Decisive/hesitant

Keep in mind that everyone is on a continuum when it comes to personality traits. Most of us are not 100 percent any of these. Therefore it is essential to look beyond the label, both in ourselves and in our partners.

For example, on a scale of introversion/extroversion, where do you and your spouse each fall, and what areas of extroversion/introversion do you share?

Introvert————Ambivert————Extrovert

We're all a confluence of all ten of these personality traits (and many more). In addition, we may find ourselves near one end of the spectrum with a spouse and near the other end of the spectrum in a different relationship.

As you look over the tips in this chapter, my hope is that some will resonate with you. And if not, I hope that these tips will serve as an impetus to help you to develop tips that will work for you.

1. Spender/Saver

Tap into Completion

SPENDER. What does my "saver" partner add to the marriage?

- Security through boundaries; often has finger on the pulse as to budgeting
- Can influence spender to delay gratification, in promise of better life later on
- Feeling of wealth through saving

SAVER. What does my spender partner add to our marriage?

- More fun/spontaneity
- Graciousness, e.g., picking up the bill or buying gifts
- Generates a feeling of abundance by enjoying the moment

Accept and Allow Tips

SPENDER

1. You equate spending with freedom; your spouse equates saving with reality (for example, saving for a rainy day). Your spouse is not trying to curtail your freedom, but rather pursuing your mutual security. Trying to keep this in mind will help you to reframe your spouse's attitude in a positive light.

2. Your spouse puts a greater emphasis on later, while you are more focused on now. Both are important.

3. You value freedom; your spouse is concerned about your *future* freedom.

4. Your spouse looks at money as potential for future freedom, while you might put a higher value on freedom in the moment.

5. The saver is *frightened* of not having enough money (later on); this is a valid fear.

SAVER

1. You equate saving with reality; your spouse equates spending with freedom. Your spouse is not trying to deplete your savings, but rather sees money as a vehicle to acquire things of value. Try to keep this in mind in order to reframe your spouse's attitude in a positive light.

2. Your spouse puts more weight on now, while you put more weight on later. Both are important.

3. Although you might view money as potential for future freedom, your spouse feels constricted by your futuristic perspective because he or she holds freedom in the moment as a higher value.

4. For spenders, money is valuable because it is the means to acquire an object; for a saver, money is valuable because it

achieves security. It is important to keep this distinction in mind, in order to be more understanding of your spender spouse.

Action Tips

SPENDER

1. Be a spender but be transparent. The worst thing for your marriage is to be a hidden spender. The AICPA (American Institute of Certified Public Accountants) recommends that you set up an agreement that 80 percent of what you spend needs approval from your spouse, with 100 percent transparency; the other 20 percent doesn't need approval.

2. Watch impulsivity. A good rule is not to bring up buying a big ticket item on your first encounter with the item. Delay the purchase, then find the middle ground. For example, try the "we" solution: we'll buy on credit once we have three-quarters of the price.

3. Put the marriage before the purchase. Say to yourself, "I can buy this." Then ask yourself, "But how will this purchase affect the relationship?"

4. Before making a proposal for spending, validate the saver's position.

5. If necessary, bringing in a mutually agreed-upon third party as advisor, arbitrator, or coach can work wonders – especially regarding recurrent arguments or major purchases.

SAVER

1. Set up an agreement for spending: the AICPA (American Institute of Certified Public Accountants) recommends that you set up an agreement that 80 percent of what your spouse spends

needs approval from you, with 100 percent transparency; the other 20 percent doesn't need approval.

2. Yes, it is important to differentiate between wants and needs, but keep in mind that not all wants are irrelevant. Be careful not to diminish the value of your partner's wants.

3. Put the marriage before the savings. Ask yourself, "If we don't buy this, what will the effect be on the relationship?"

4. Before making a proposal for saving, validate the spender's position.

5. If necessary, bringing in a mutually agreed-upon third party as advisor, arbitrator, or coach can work wonders –especially regarding recurrent arguments or major purchases.

2. Extrovert/Introvert

Tap into Completion

EXTROVERT. What does my introvert partner add to our marriage?

- Higher value of privacy
- A more grounded, internally focused relationship
- More opportunity for introspection

INTROVERT. What does my extrovert partner add to our marriage?

- Social interaction; feeling connected to more of the people around us
- May introduce more fun and lightness
- Generates excitement through sharing life experiences

Accept and Allow Tips

EXTROVERT

1. Your spouse derives his or her oxygen and vitality from connection to self and private time with you. His or her need for your time and attention is truly a compliment, because *you* are the person your spouse lets into his or her world.

2. Socially, you may be the center of your spouse's social life. If you're spending so much time with others, it can be hurtful. Your spouse needs to know that he or she is your priority. You can show it with the quality time (hint: this means uninterrupted) you give him or her.

3. The introvert does not perceive your opting to spend time with others as a choice of "them" *and* your spouse but rather as a choice of "them" *or* him or her.

INTROVERT

1. Your spouse derives his or her oxygen and vitality from connection to the outside world. Keeping this in mind will help you to accept and allow.

2. Your spouse has a social network that may carry with it certain demands. Typically, such a network carries with it social obligations that can be complex.

3. For the extrovert, it's not seen as a choice of "them" *or* you but rather as a choice of "them" *and* you.

Action Tips

EXTROVERT

1. When planning activities, whenever possible make a joint decision regarding location, environment, venue, etc.

2. Many introverts do not appreciate surprises. In general it's best to give your spouse some advance notice regarding any expected changes in plans or life in general.

3. Introverts tend to be very sensitive to privacy. If you ever want to reprimand your spouse, do so privately.

4. Try to divide tasks in accordance with your tendencies toward extroversion or introversion, e.g., the extrovert might go to the supermarket, while the introvert might do the bills.

INTROVERT

1. When planning activities, whenever possible make a joint decision regarding location, environment, venue, etc.

2. Many extroverts appreciate surprises. If this is true of your spouse, think of a thoughtful way to surprise him or her.

3. The social arena is of extreme importance to your spouse. If you can find a way to compliment him or her in public, it would be very appreciated. Help your spouse to shine!

4. Try to divide tasks in accordance with your tendencies toward extroversion or introversion, e.g., the extrovert might go to the supermarket, while the introvert might do the bills.

3. Organized/Not-So-Organized

Tap into Completion

ORGANIZED. What does my not-so-organized partner add to our marriage?

Often, people who are not organized bring the following personality traits to the marriage:

- A greater tolerance for external disorder (e.g., a kid's messy room)

- A greater ability to improvise and think out of the box when life throws a curve ball
- A certain kind of easygoing flexibility

NOT-SO-ORGANIZED. What does my organized partner add to our marriage?

- Organization
- A strong awareness of and ability to implement structure
- A heightened awareness of boundaries

Accept and Allow Tips

ORGANIZED

1. Sometimes, people who are not organized make a decision *not* to organize their things, in order to spend their (limited) time doing things they consider more valuable. It might not be as haphazard as it seems.

2. Some people work from a place of chaos because it supports their creativity and a natural state of flow.

3. Sometimes, letting go and allowing things to step out of structure is healthy. Is it possible to let some of your spouse's mellowness into your life?

4. Tolerance goes both ways. Organized people struggle to tolerate what they perceive as their spouses' sabotage of their organization. People who are not organized struggle to tolerate their spouses' perceived obsession with organization.

NOT-SO-ORGANIZED

1. Sometimes, people are only able to be organized in their minds once they are organized in their environments (e.g., I can't begin to work at my desk until I organize my desktop).

Your spouse might not be able to think straight when things are disorganized.

2. Organized people often see organization as a value; therefore, it is very dear to them. As a result, a spouse's disorganization is often experienced as an intrusion on one's very being (since space is shared) and can be painful to endure.

3. Some organization of your disorganization can be helpful. Is it possible to allow some of your spouse's organization into your life?

4. Tolerance goes both ways. Organized people struggle to tolerate what they perceive as their spouses' sabotage of their organization. People who are not organized often struggle to tolerate their spouses' perceived obsession with organization.

Action Tips for Organized and Not-So-Organized

1. Agree upon creating a personal space for each spouse that can be as organized or as cluttered as each spouse desires. This could be a small or big space depending on the resources and needs of the couple.

2. For the organized spouse: What is the lowest standard of neatness that you could tolerate without feeling an urge to comment or correct? For the spouse who is not organized: What level of order would not impede on your creativity/freedom and wouldn't be perceived as oppressive? Based on the answers to the above questions, try to find a compromise you could both live with.

3. Organization of time (i.e., time management) is extremely important and deserves its own book; it is not within the scope of this book to deal with this subject. If you have disagreements around the issue, search for resources to help you come to productive agreements that work for you.

4. Emotional/Intellectual

Tap into Completion

EMOTIONAL. What does my intellectual partner add to our marriage?

- An added component of consistency and/or dependability (lean on me)
- An antidote to emotional overwhelm (because he/she is not as emotional), which can help you regulate more when you need it

INTELLECTUAL. What does my emotional partner add to our marriage?

- Stimulates the emotional side of the relationship and helps it to be expressed more overtly; initiates emotional communication, thus opening the door for more expression of your feelings in the marriage
- Possibly more playfulness, which typically brings more color and vitality to the relationship (e.g., facial expression, body language, tone of voice); can provide important emotional connection needed by children

Accept and Allow Tips

EMOTIONAL

1. The intellectual is not trying to reject your feelings or discredit your perspective. Thinking is your spouse's "go to" place, because it's his or her natural way of processing and approaching issues in life.
2. The approach of the intellectual and the emotional person are both relevant at different times and can be an unbeatable com-

bination. Sometimes, the intellectual's logic and objectivity could lead to a shortcut to the solution in dealing with a child or decision making.

3. Although your intellectual spouse of course has feelings, he or she is not as comfortable in the emotional realm as you are and may not be able to identify the feelings as clearly and readily as you can. Be patient and try to understand that emotions are not a comfort zone for your spouse.

INTELLECTUAL

1. Many people in the world operate from an emotional base. Your spouse is preparing you for more successful interactions with all of these people (who might even be your own children, parents, or coworkers).

2. The approach of the intellectual and emotional person are both relevant at different times and an unbeatable combination. Sometimes, an emotional person's intuition could provide critical information that you wouldn't arrive at on your own, for example in dealing with a child or decision making.

3. Although everyone has a thinking process, the cognitive realm is not your spouse's "go to" place. Approaching an issue analytically typically does not come as easily to your spouse as it does to you.

Action Tips

EMOTIONAL

1. Intellectuals appreciate acknowledgement of their thinking ability and thought process. Express appreciation for this.

2. In general, be direct when communicating with an intellectual. Put the facts on the table. The less hinting, the better. And try

to keep your message calm, focused and short (you might need
to practice this…it's a skill!).

3. Try not to be put off by an intellectual's presentation of facts. It
might seem cold. Try not to personalize this; it's just the way
an intellectual's brain works.

INTELLECTUAL

1. Are there times or situations in which it's easier for you to
access your more emotional self? (For example with children, in nature, while doing hobbies, etc.). If possible, share
these times with your spouse. It will create an ease in your
relationship.

2. Try to make the effort to identify and *acknowledge* the feelings
of your partner. "I think you're frustrated right now and I get
that." Stepping out of your comfort zone in this way will be
very helpful. Especially when there is conflict, attempting to
tune in to what your spouse is feeling (and reflecting it back)
will go a long way.

3. Never underestimate the power of listening. Often, emotional
people need to express their feelings without being solution
oriented. Check in while you listen. Just asking "How can
I be helpful here?" can direct your conversation in a more
productive way.

5. Faster Paced/Slower Paced

Tap into Completion

FASTER PACED. What does my slower partner add to our marriage?

• The probability of making fewer mistakes – there is less chance
of stumbling when you slow down and challenge impulsivity

- A reminder to slow down and smell the coffee, to take advantage of the moment

SLOWER PACED. What does my faster partner add to our marriage?

- More energy, more vitality, and for some, more spontaneity
- Greater productivity and adventure

Accept and Allow Tips

FASTER PACED

1. Imagine if there were only fast music in the world. Slow music adds texture, emotion, and depth.
2. A slower person's perspective in life is "Life is short; every moment has to be savored." A faster person's perspective in life is "Life is short, don't waste any time." Both perspectives are valuable.

SLOWER PACED

1. Imagine if there were only slow music in the world. Fast music adds rhythm, excitement, and momentum.
2. A faster person's perspective in life is "Life is short; don't waste any time." A slower person's perspective in life is "Life is short; every moment has to be savored." Both are valuable.

Action Tips

FASTER PACED

1. Carry a book or project around with you so that you can be productive while waiting for your spouse.
2. Think about how annoying it is to be told to "Slow down." It's important to recognize that from your partner's perspective, it's equally as hard to be told to "Hurry up."

SLOWER PACED

1. It is difficult for a faster person to slow down. Sometimes it really helps to empathize with this struggle by saying something like, "I know my speed is hard for you...I really get it. But please understand that I really am going as fast as I can."

2. Think about how annoying it is to be told to "Hurry up." It's important to recognize that from your partner's perspective, it's equally as hard to be told to "Slow down."

6. More Affectionate/Less Affectionate

Note: Although the sexual relationship in marriage is of utmost importance, it is beyond the scope of this book. This section refers only to casual affection, outside the bedroom.

Tap into Completion

LESS AFFECTIONATE. What might my more affectionate partner add to our marriage?

- More expressed warmth and playfulness
- More emotional connection

MORE AFFECTIONATE. What might my less affectionate partner add to our marriage?

- More allowing of individual and personal space
- Respect for boundaries, rules, and structure

Accept and Allow Tips

MORE AFFECTIONATE

1. Although you might equate physical touch with closeness and warmth, your partner may not, to the same degree. When your

spouse is not touching you, it is not a rejection of you; it is a reflection of his or her need for physical space.

2. Although you might equate love with demonstrative physical affection, your partner may not. It's important not to assume that your spouse loves you any less. Some people feel that the reality of their love is an internal thing and does not need constant external expression. Keep in mind that there are many ways to express love; not everyone speaks the same "love language."

LESS AFFECTIONATE

1. Your spouse may equate physical touch with emotional closeness. He or she is not trying to suffocate you. An inadequate amount of physical touch may feel like a rejection to your spouse. It is important to be aware of this.

2. You might see the small expressions of casual physical affection as an "extra" in a marriage, but your partner might see it as a reassurance of your love. Some people need that momentary confirmation more often. It's important not to assume that it's a function of insecurity, but rather your spouse's nature.

Action Tips

MORE AFFECTIONATE

1. Think about the possibility that your spouse authentically might need less affection than you do. Try to hold back at times; this might open up the opportunity for him or her to initiate. For example, try not to sit or stand in a way that "corners" your partner (physically or emotionally). This will give him or her the space to initiate ... and affection freely offered may then mean a lot more to you.

2. When your spouse demonstrates affection, take it in and express appreciation – even if it isn't the type or amount of affection you crave.

LESS AFFECTIONATE

1. Look for more opportunities to initiate affection, when possible.

2. Sometimes you just won't be in the mood to be touchy-feely. However, it's important to look for other ways to make him or her feel loved and appreciated. Verbal affection can go a long way (compliments, expressions of appreciation). Also, nonverbal expressions of care such as listening, a smile, or a wink can fill in the void.

7. Optimist/Pessimist

Tap into Completion

OPTIMIST. What does my pessimist partner add to our marriage?

- Aligns more with what is rather than with what could be; may be better at examining and weeding out options that lead to a loss of time, energy, or money, etc.
- May be able to help you direct your positivity to the most appropriate areas, so as to avoid naive misdirected positivity

PESSIMIST. What does my optimist partner add to our marriage?

- More positive energy
- Can stretch you out of the box, which may free you from a limiting perspective

Accept and Allow Tips

OPTIMIST

1. Think about balanced optimism as a goal. Be careful of extreme

optimism: the goal is "effective optimism," which means not being afraid of hearing a realist's perspective.

2. Try not to label your spouse as a defeatist. This closes your mind to a positive influence your spouse might have in your life; your spouse just might be able to help you fine-tune your optimism.

3. You will come across a lot of pessimists in your life. Learning to deal with your spouse's pessimism will prepare you to interact successfully with other realists (some of whom might be your own children).

PESSIMIST

1. Be careful of extreme pessimism. Sometimes the optimist is actually right.

2. Try not to label your spouse as a hopeless or naive dreamer. This closes your mind to a positive influence he or she could have in your life; your spouse just might be able to help you to expand your horizons.

3. You will come across a lot of optimists in your life. Learning to deal with your spouse's optimism will prepare you to interact successfully with other optimists (some of whom might be your own children).

Action Tips

OPTIMIST

1. Dream big...but don't be afraid to check in with reality. When your spouse expresses an idea or reaction, take the time to consider his or her perspective.

2. One of the greatest determinants of happiness is having expectations that are grounded in reality. Your spouse can help you decipher whether your expectations are grounded in reality. It's easier to change your expectations than to change reality.

3. Remind yourself of how much more grounded you've become because you're married to a pessimist. Keep this clearly in mind next time you decide that your spouse is a "party pooper."

PESSIMIST

1. Take your spouse's optimism seriously. Convey this by taking the time to consider his or her perspective and communicating that you are doing so.

2. Some pessimists have a tendency to catastrophize. Be careful not to turn one negative into "everything is negative." The tendency to focus exclusively on the problem and to catastrophize could keep one from actually finding a solution.

3. There is a difference between critical and analytical. Sometimes, the difference is in the tone. If you are able to stay analytical (which tends to be more discerning and accepting than a critical point of view), you have a better chance of being heard by your spouse.

8. Doer/"Be-er"

Tap into Completion

DOER. What does my "be-er" partner add to our marriage?

- More awareness of the here and now, enjoyment of the moment
- Greater sense of peace and tranquility, because they typically don't need to run from one thing to the next

"BE-ER." What does my doer partner add to our marriage?

- Greater efficiency; things really get done
- Often brings initiative to the family and gets things going, e.g., planning a vacation or a new project (you wouldn't be able to

appreciate the great moment on that mountain or in the forest if your spouse didn't plan the vacation)

Accept and Allow Tips

DOER

1. A "be-er" needs to connect (to another person ... or to him- or herself ... or to a moment ... or to an event, etc.) for a sense of well-being – especially on vacation!
2. The energy you bring into the home will inevitably affect your spouse. Your "be-er" spouse might have difficulty relaxing until you settle down.

"BE-ER"

1. A doer's confidence is often associated with accomplishing – even while on vacation! This is why he or she is probably busy planning a hectic itinerary for vacations, rather than looking forward to just sitting back.
2. "Be-ers" often feel ignored by doers because of the "task focus" of the doer. Try not to take the doer's focus personally. (However, if you see that you are ignored, speak up about it.

Action Tips

DOER

1. Be careful not to pack so much into your day that you have no time to connect and build relationships. Sometimes a doer's list is so long that his or her spouse feels the need to make an appointment, just to talk.
2. Keep your finger on the pulse so as to avoid falling into the overfunctioner/underfunctioner pattern (see below). Even if

you are the dominant person on a project/activity/situation the two of you are dealing with, look for ways to include your spouse.

3. Plan activities and vacations that include both doing and being.

"BE-ER"

1. Express appreciation when your doer spouse takes care of the things you are not inclined to do. Feel the relief… and express it.

2. Keep your finger on the pulse so as to avoid falling into the overfunctioner/underfunctioner pattern (see below). Even if your spouse is the dominant person on a project/activity/situation the two of you are dealing with, look for ways to assist.

3. Plan activities and vacations that include both being and doing.

9. Very Giving/More Restrained

Tap into Completion

VERY GIVING. What does my more restrained partner add to our marriage?

- Boundaries and rules that can help direct your giving in a more productive way
- Has an easier time setting limits/saying no (which is important sometimes)
- Typically has an important contribution when it comes to disciplining children

MORE RESTRAINED. What does my very giving partner add to our marriage?

- More expressed compassion
- More of a sense of contribution and belonging to a community

- Typically has an important contribution when it comes to creating warm, affectionate relationships with children

Accept and Allow Tips

VERY GIVING

1. In order for productive giving to happen, there need to be boundaries, rules, and structure. Boundaries can be compared to seat belts and brakes in a car. Understanding this helps you gain appreciation for your spouse's boundaries (instead of seeing them as selfish and heartless).

2. Although rigid boundaries can create disconnection, excessive giving can make you feel depleted and overextended.

3. Your restrained spouse can reel you in sometimes and help set priorities, when your giving takes you away from your marriage and kids.

MORE RESTRAINED

1. Giving is absolutely essential in relationships; it is one of the most important expressions of love and is the most important ingredient for rejuvenation of love. Internalizing this helps you gain appreciation for your spouse's giving.

2. Although rules are important, too many rules can choke and destroy. Your giving spouse can help you monitor your boundaries so that they are not harsh and/or overly restrictive (within your family and in your life in general).

3. Even though givers might go overboard at times, their giving is usually an important expression of connection and appreciation and is very closely connected to their inner core and self-image. Keeping this in mind can help you establish boundaries more gently.

Action Tips

VERY GIVING

1. Keep your finger on the pulse (of your giving) by asking yourself the following questions:
   A. Is your giving coming from a "people-pleasing" place?
   B. Are you prioritizing your family?
   C. Is your giving creating a dependency of sorts?
2. Are you taking care of yourself? Self-care is essential for a healthy giver; be careful of falling into martyr mode.
3. Are you giving your spouse what he or she actually needs? Or are you giving your spouse what *you* need, or giving without focus just because you "need to give"?

MORE RESTRAINED

1. Keep your finger on the pulse (of your boundaries) by asking yourself the following questions:
   A. Are you boundaries too rigid or harsh?
   B. Are you making sure that your boundaries are established in a gentle enough way so that they can be heard and implemented?
2. If your boundaries are making you isolated or resentful of others, how can you stretch yourself to be more giving?
3. Look for areas of your spouse's giving where you can partner/join with your spouse.

10. Decisive/Hesitant

Tap into Completion

DECISIVE. What does my hesitant partner add to our marriage?
- Attentive deliberation

- Can save you from jumping into a decision you'll regret
- Helps you make a better decision by causing you to explain it

HESITANT. What does my decisive partner add to our marriage?
- Closure and resolution
- Relief at your times of indecision; lessens the feeling of overwhelm
- Gets things going and gives direction (resists inertia)

Accept and Allow Tips

DECISIVE

1. Your hesitant spouse is reflecting. Keep in mind that as frustrating as his or her indecisiveness is for you, it might possibly be more frustrating for your spouse.

2. Your hesitant spouse is most likely operating from fear of being wrong. Pay attention to that fear; it might be exactly what you need to make a more balanced decision. His or her indecisiveness is really a signal to you for caution (it's a yellow light, not a red light).

3. Your hesitant spouse is not expressing lack of trust in you. It's not that he or she doesn't believe in you; typically it is the decision that is being contemplated, not the decider.

HESITANT

1. If you create a vacuum by not being a decider (taking a back seat with decisions), accept and understand the fact that your decisive partner will naturally fill the vacuum.

2. Imagine if your spouse agreed with your hesitations, every time you were indecisive. Where would this get you? Remembering this will be a great source of appreciation.

3. You advocate reflection; your spouse advocates solution. This is a winning combination. Therefore, there are times to accept and allow your spouse's momentum, and not to resist.

Action Tips (For Joint Decisions)

DECISIVE

1. Before rushing into a decision or suggestion, it's important to check in with your spouse.

2. If your spouse asks you to make the decision alone, beware of falling into the overfunctioner/underfunctioner pattern (see below).

3. When your hesitant partner voices concerns, make sure to *validate* them before suggesting your own (so that you're not discounting your spouse).

4. Sometimes, what a hesitant person needs is just more time to reflect. Although this will demand more patience from you, allowing your spouse more time for reflection could pay off for both of you.

HESITANT

1. Remember that *not* making a decision is an action – and possibly an indication to your spouse to take over. If you let your spouse make the decision, be careful not to be resentful of it.

2. If you forfeit your vote on a decision, beware of falling into the overfunctioner/underfunctioner pattern (see below).

3. Make it clear that your hesitations are about the subject at hand, not a reflection on your spouse's decision-making abilities.

4. When your partner is pushing for a solution, try not to take it personally. He or she has a strong need for closure; for many decisive people, it is painful to wait and deliberate when it comes to making a decision.

Overfunctioners and Underfunctioners

When it comes to relationships, it is essential to clarify a very common pattern. In many marriages, there is a tendency for one spouse to overfunction in one area (such as with children), while the other spouse might overfunction in another area (for example with career). This could work well for a couple, as long as both parties agree on the pattern.

However, trouble sets in when one spouse starts to overfunction in all or most areas while the other spouse starts to underfunction. Often, it looks like one party is the super responsible hero while the other party is the irresponsible villain. Although there are instances where this is true, most situations are not this simplistic.

Instead, these couples are doing the dance of the overfunctioner and underfunctioner. What really is going on is:

- The overfunctioner is very efficient and typically has a hard time delegating responsibility.
- The underfunctioner is less efficient and less inclined to initiate (but is not necessarily irresponsible).

The overfunctioner/underfunctioner pattern starts to snowball when the spouse who is more "on top of things" (at least in a particular area) steps in and takes on more and more responsibility; the other spouse feels irrelevant, redundant, incapable and/or overwhelmed, and moves away from responsibility. Thus, the gap widens between them.

The overfunctioner starts to think:

- "I always have to compensate for my partner's lack of responsibility."
- "My spouse has some real issues; I'm exhausted from trying to solve them."

The Underfunctioner starts to think:

- "My spouse is controlling and overbearing; I really need some space."
- "My spouse has to be in charge and is ruining my life."

OR

- "I'm just not capable; I guess I can't do very much."

The truth underlying the overfunctioner's and underfunctioner's behavior is as follows:

Overfunctioner	
Subjective Truth	**Objective Truth**
I am trapped in over-responsibility because my spouse is a loser.	I am trapped in over-responsibility that is partially self-made.
My spouse is a loser, pathetic, and depends on me to carry him/her.	Part of the reason my spouse is being so irresponsible is as a reaction to my over-responsibility.
I have no choice but to continue being the hero.	I need to learn how to share and delegate responsibilities.

Underfunctioner	
Subjective Truth	**Objective Truth**
I am helpless and am stuck in under-responsibility.	I may feel helpless and stuck in under-responsibility, but I can do something to step out of this.
My spouse is a control freak.	Part of the reason my partner is stuck in over-responsibility is as a reaction to my under-responsibility.

Subjective Truth	Objective Truth
I'll just try to hang in here and bear my overbearing spouse.	I need to learn how to work with my spouse to see how I can take on more responsibility.

If you and your spouse are stuck in the underfunctioner/over-functioner dynamic, here's how to work toward a more balanced relationship:

1. If both spouses are aware of this pattern and are willing to work on it, pick one specific issue and decide how each spouse will respectively take one step up (for the underfunctioner) and one step down (for the overfunctioner).

2. If only one spouse is on board, take one step up or down, without expecting your spouse to notice. Repeat this a few times. Afterwards, you can inform your spouse (in a nonjudgmental or demanding way) that you are working on becoming more responsible or less overbearing, as applicable. Even if your spouse does not change his or her behavior to reciprocate, by virtue of your behaving in a different way on a consistent basis, there will be a shift in the relationship.

It is important to consider that sometimes, an underfunctioner has an objective disability, whether physically (such as injury from a stroke or complications of diabetes) or emotionally (for example, suffering from severe mood swings). In situations such as these, it is expected that this spouse underfunctions. However, even in situations like this, it's essential to make sure that the underfunctioner dynamic does not go farther than it needs to (thus taking over the general dynamic of the marriage). People with disabilities still have plenty of areas in which to shine.

Unhappy Compatibility

Ironically, the biggest challenge in Andrea and Dylan's relationship wasn't their personality differences – but rather their similarities. Despite the fact that they're both financially astute (Andrea has a master's degree in economics and Dylan is a highly successful businessman), neither of them went into the marriage with strong *personal* finance skills. "When it comes to money management, Andrea and I are in trouble," Dylan said. "Neither of us knows how to save money. We waste everything: the more we make, the more we spend. And we have no idea where our money is going. We look back at the month and say, 'Well, this is something we really needed, this is a necessity ...' In a marriage, it's better if one spouse is very strong in this area, but neither of us is."

Dylan and Andrea, like many other couples, share a common personality trait that happens to be a struggle for each one of them, individually. They are both spenders. Other couples are both messy; others are procrastinators.

Jeffrey, one of the men from our relationship study, said:

JEFFREY: We are both sensitive. This commonality has its advantages; we can be more sensitive to each other and are both caring to others. As a matter of fact, we open our home to many people who need a place to crash; we just care about people very deeply. However, the down side is that we are both very sensitive about ourselves and can get hurt very easily. What helps me in our interactions is to take a step back and feel compassion toward her. I work hard at validating her and accepting her.

One way we can get trapped in our comfort zone is when we *share* a personality trait that is challenging to our marriage (in Dylan and Andrea's case, it's avoiding financial reality). This type of commonality tends to reinforce unproductive patterns, trapping us further into our comfort zones. Or alternatively, we might end up teaming up (subconsciously) with our spouses to resist the important change that is needed.

When the Challenge Is a Personality Similarity

Here are some practical tips for couples who share a personality trait that is a challenge to their marriages.

- Find a role model for the behavior you mutually believe represents balanced behavior. Take small, steady steps toward reaching that goal. Or, find a third person who can serve as a mentor, coach, or therapist to help both of you establish an objective goal.

- Instead of beating your spouse up for having a similar trait (it can be very hard to see ourselves in another person), celebrate the fact that you share a common struggle – you can actually bond over this! Also, be careful not to beat yourselves up as a couple, saying things like "We are so messed up" or "Our marriage is a joke."

- If one of you gets ahead of the other, lead the way, but do not chastise. For example, if you are both quitting smoking and one of you is succeeding, take the lead with compassion. When we are growing, it is all too easy to judge others who might not be growing as fast (or whom we perceive as not growing as fast).

- If your spouse does not want to work on this mutual challenge, don't underestimate the effect of your efforts to change. Focus on your own individual work and celebrate your own growth. Your actions will create ripple effects in the marriage, since marriage is a system.

Appendices

Appendix A

Research Methodology

The examples and interviews in this book are based on a research study comprised of:

- 400 surveys generated by Qualtrics throughout the USA (Qualtrics provided a convenience sampling of men and women; the participants had to be married for at least one year)
- 53 personal interviews, provided through snowball sampling, in eight different countries: the USA, England, India, Russia, Argentina, South Africa, Israel, and Australia

Questionnaire: Personality Differences in Marriage

Breakdown of the participants in the survey:

- 200 participants were female, 200 were male
- Age range: 20–69 years old
- 268 participants were in first marriages
- 98 participants were in second marriages
- 20 participants were in third marriages
- 9 participants were in fourth marriages
- 5 participants were in fifth marriages

Participants in the survey received the following letter.

Dear married participant,

Personality differences are a given in every relationship. Each marriage holds a unique combination of personality traits. I am surveying hundreds of married people to assess the impact of personality differences within marriages. Knowing the way in which you, in particular, experience your marriage would be a very valuable contribution to our study. I hope to enrich our understanding of marriage dynamics based on this research. As a result, I hope that my new findings will make a profound contribution to the existing literature and to the population at large.

To participate in this important study, please take fifteen minutes to complete the questionnaire. Your response to this questionnaire will be confidential, and your specific answers will not be identified with you personally. (Only summary information from all respondents completing the questionnaires will be reported, so your answers cannot be connected to you in any way.) Your answers will only be identified by a code and not by your name or contact information.

You are under no obligation to be part of this study, but I hope that you volunteer to provide your valuable input. The results of this study will assist many other married individuals to understand and use their marital differences to enhance their lives.

All information asked for in this questionnaire deals with commonly discussed attitudes and behaviors and should not cause any physical, legal, emotional, social, or financial harm.

Thank you for your cooperation,

                                                        Chana Levitan, MSc

Below is the survey that was administered to four hundred people throughout the United States.

Section A: Personal Information

A1. What is your gender? M __ F __

A2. How many years have you been married? _____

A3. What is your year of birth? _____
What is your spouse's year of birth? _____

A4. Number of prior marriages: _____

Section B: Similar Personality Traits

B1. Identify the most important personality trait that you share with your spouse: _____

B2. When in your relationship did you notice this similar trait?
__ While dating   __ Recently
__ Early in our marriage   __ Other time, please specify:

_____

B3. Identify another important personality trait that you share with your spouse: _____

B4. At what point in your relationship did you notice this second similar trait?
__ While dating   __ Recently
__ Early in our marriage   __ Other time, please specify:

_____

Section C: Difference in Personality Traits

C1. Identify a major personality difference between you and your spouse: _____

C2. To what degree do you think your spouse would agree that this is a personality difference?

__ Totally agree	__ Totally disagree
__ Somewhat agree	__ Somewhat disagree
__ Slightly agree	__ Slightly disagree

C3. At what point in your relationship did you notice this personality difference?

__ During the dating process	__ Recently
__ Early in the marriage	__ Other, please specify: _____

_____

C4. On the whole, rate the impact this personality difference has had on your marriage: _____

0	1	2	3	4	5	6	7	8	9	10
DETRIMENTAL										BENEFICIAL

C5. If you think this personality difference is beneficial, what are the benefits?

__ I have been forced to work on my patience.

__ Exposure to my spouse's difference has pushed me to work on myself in this area.

__ I have been better able to understand people similar to my spouse.

__ I have come to appreciate this trait in general.

__ There are no benefits.

__ Other, please specify: _____

C6. If you think this personality difference is detrimental, what are the negative consequences?

___ I have become less patient.

___ I have given up on trying to bridge the gap.

___ I am less tolerant of others similar to my spouse.

___ I have come to despise this trait in general.

___ There are no negative consequences.

___ Other, please specify: _____

Section D: Personality Differences Part 2

D1. What is another personality difference between you and your spouse? _____

D2. To what degree do you think your spouse would agree that this is a personality difference?

___ Totally agree   ___ Totally disagree

___ Somewhat agree   ___ Somewhat disagree

___ Slightly agree   ___ Slightly disagree

D3. At what point in your relationship did you notice this personality difference?

___ During the dating process ___ Recently

___ Early in the marriage   ___ Other, please specify: _____

_____

D4. On the whole, rate the impact this difference has had on your marriage: _____

0	1	2	3	4	5	6	7	8	9	10
DETRIMENTAL										BENEFICIAL

D5. If you think this personality difference is beneficial, what are the benefits?

___ I have been forced to work on my patience.

___ Being exposed to my spouse's difference has pushed me to work on myself in this area.

___ I have been better able to understand people similar to my spouse.

___ I have come to appreciate this trait in general.

___ There are no benefits.

___ Other, please specify: _____

D6. If you think this personality difference is detrimental, what are the negative consequences?

___ I have become less patient.

___ I have given up on trying to bridge the gap.

___ I am less tolerant of others similar to my spouse.

___ I have come to despise this trait in general.

___ There are no negative consequences.

___ Other, please specify: _____

Section E: Interactions within the Marriage

E1. When encountering difficulties in your marriage, have you ever made an effort to change your spouse? Yes ____ No ____ (If the answer is no, skip to E3.)

E2. If you answered yes, rate the directness of your effort: _____

0	1	2	3	4	5	6	7	8	9	10

NOT DIRECT AT ALL   SOMEWHAT DIRECT   EXTREMELY DIRECT

How successful were your efforts?

___ Very successful

___ Moderately successful

__ Minimally successful
__ Unsuccessful
__ Other, please specify: _____

E3. Which of the following, if any, has been the most helpful in dealing with the difficulties? (If more than one, please rank, with 1 being most helpful):

__ Clergy guidance   __ I worked it out directly with my spouse

__ Professional guidance   __ I worked on the difficulties myself

__ A book/lecture   __ Meditation
__ A mentor or role model __ Prayer
__ Other, please specify: _____

E4. What was the most compelling personality trait that led you to marry your spouse? _____

To what degree do you have this trait within yourself? _____

0	1	2	3	4	5	6	7	8	9	10
NOT AT ALL		EQUAL TO MY SPOUSE				MORE THAN MY SPOUSE				

E5. What are your five most important values? Choose from the following values and/or list your own:

Community Service	Efficiency	Loyalty	Equality	Other
Communication	Spirituality	Honesty	Kindness	Other
Health consciousness	Ambition	Self-control	Justice	Other
Trustworthiness	Religion	Commitment	Family minded	Other
Being knowledgeable	Work ethic	Purpose	Responsibility	Other

E6. From your perspective, what are your spouse's five most important values? Choose from the following values and/or list your own:

Community Service	Efficiency	Loyalty	Equality	Other
Communication	Spirituality	Honesty	Kindness	Other
Health consciousness	Ambition	Self-control	Justice	Other
Trustworthiness	Religion	Commitment	Family minded	Other
Being knowledgeable	Work ethic	Purpose	Responsibility	Other

E7. If you have values in common with your spouse, what is the impact of the similar values on your marriage? _____

0	1	2	3	4	5	6	7	8	9	10
DETRIMENTAL									BENEFICIAL	

E8. If you have values that differ from your spouse's, what is the impact of the difference in values on your marriage? _____

0	1	2	3	4	5	6	7	8	9	10
DETRIMENTAL									BENEFICIAL	

E9. What is your religious affiliation?

___ Christian   ___ Buddhist

___ Jewish   ___ None

___ Muslim   ___ Other, please specify: _____

E10. What is your spouse's religious affiliation?

___ Christian   ___ Buddhist

___ Jewish   ___ None

___ Muslim   ___ Other, please specify: _____

E11. How many years of education do you have? _____

E12. How many years of education does your spouse have? ____

E13. Which state in the USA do you live in? _____

Personal Interviews

Breakdown of the participants in the personal interviews:

- 28 participants were female, 25 were male
- Age range: 27–70 years old
- 46 participants were presently married in first marriages, married at least one year
- 1 participant was in a second marriage, married for three years
- 2 participants were in third marriages, married for over three years
- 1 participant was in a fourth marriage, married for twenty years
- 3 participants were divorced but presently in serious relationships moving toward marriage (these three interviews concentrated only on what transpired in the marriage before the divorce)

The following questions were addressed to the participants in my international personal interviews:

1. What is your age?
2. How long have you been married?
3. Is this your first marriage? If not, how many times were you married before?
4. What is your country of permanent residence?
5. Before we explore the personality differences between you and your spouse, can you name one personality similarity?
6. Can you name another personality similarity?

7. What is one major personality difference between you and your spouse?

8. At what point in your relationship did you notice this personality difference?

9. Are there any challenges that you've experienced due to this personality difference? If so, what are those challenges?

10. How have you dealt with these challenges?

11. Have you tried to change your spouse? If so, in what ways?

12. Are there any benefits from this personality difference?

13. Can you name another personality difference between you and your spouse?

14. At what point in your relationship did you notice this personality difference?

15. Are there any challenges that you've experienced due to this personality difference? If so, what are those challenges?

16. How have you dealt with these challenges?

17. Are there any benefits from this personality difference?

18. What originally attracted you to your spouse?

19. How many years of education do you have? Does your spouse have?

20. Optional: Do you and/or your spouse have a religious affiliation? If so, please specify which religion you adhere to or identify with.

Appendix B

Additional Information on the Downward Spiral

Additional Information for Step Two, Annoyance and Disrespect

According to Dr. John Gottman, a leading social science researcher, a good marriage normally needs at least a 5:1 ratio of positive to negative interactions, in order to succeed. Gottman points out that neutral is not positive, it is neutral. His research shows that divorce is predicted by an absence of positive interactions. Bottom line – neutral does not count or register as positive, although many people think it does.

An example of a neutral interaction is "Pass the salt." This interaction becomes positive when it calls forth an element of connection, such as, "Honey, could you pass the salt?"

Positive interactions are so essential because hidden annoyance does have a negative effect; at the very least, it zaps the positive out of the relationship. And although our disrespect can seem very discreet, it will nonetheless register as negative to the person on the receiving end. In addition, if you disrespect your spouse, you will teach your children to disrespect your spouse... and you. The best way to teach your kids to respect you is to respect your spouse.

Additional Information for Step Four, Comparing and Competing

Making comparisons is not always bad – actually, it can help us gauge the health and progress of our own marriages. When marriages slip into the downward spiral, however, most of the comparing is negative.

There are four steps to the negative comparison process. Before we see how the comparing process works in relationships, let's first see how it works with individuals. The first step is when a person starts to feel that he or she is not particularly special or unique. Often, we're not even aware that we're feeling this way until we find ourselves in "comparing mode." Sometimes, what sends us into this state is being face-to-face with a person we perceive as more talented, successful, beautiful, etc., than we are. This is how the four steps of negative comparing mode look on an individual level:

1. Not feeling special and unique
2. Comparing oneself
3. Feeling nullified
4. Jealousy

Here's how that might play out in an example scenario:

1. Not feeling special and unique	2. Comparing oneself	3. Feeling nullified	4. Jealousy
Mark, who isn't feeling successful at work, hears about Joey's new job.	Mark thinks, "Joey is smarter and more talented than I am."	Mark thinks, "Why can't I get it together? I was never smart."	Mark feels jealous of Joey.

We all have holes in our self-confidence. When we find ourselves stuck in "comparing mode" and/or jealousy, it's simply a signal that we have to strengthen and internalize our confidence in our uniqueness and specialness. We *all* have our particular uniqueness. The goal is to be the best version of yourself – not of someone else. The more we celebrate our personal victories, the less we compare, and the more we can create relationships that are real and meaningful. It doesn't matter if someone is indeed more talented or successful; what matters is that we're in touch with our specialness/uniqueness and that we are actualizing our own unique potential.

When it comes to relationships, comparing can be extremely corrosive. Here's how the process looks when we begin negatively comparing our marriages with others':

1. Not seeing one's spouse as special and unique
2. Comparing other people's spouses
3. Nullifying the relationship
4. Jealousy

Similar to the individual process, the first step of the process is a feeling that one's marriage or spouse is "nothing special":

My husband is nothing special.	Nancy's husband is so wonderful.	I have the worst husband out there.	I'm jealous of Nancy.

Even if we're not down on our spouses, the urge to compare and compete can overwhelm us. This is what the process can look like:

My marriage is pretty good.	Wow, Ben's marriage seems amazing. His wife is so funny.	I don't have an amazing marriage. Why doesn't my wife have a sense of humor?	I'm jealous of Ben.

This usually happens when we're not actively working on marriage improvement but are rather settling for mediocrity. When we create new, stronger bonds with our spouses, we get a high – but when that energy is missing from a relationship, it's easy to get jealous of the high we see in someone else's marriage.

The comparing and competing mentality can also play out between spouses themselves. In business or sports, a company or team must constantly choose between competition versus synergy. Sometimes, competition is what drives employees or players to exceed expectations. Other times, the only way to get results is through teamwork and drawing on the strengths of each individual therein. In marriage, synergy is the only approach that works, because when spouses compete against each other, the teamwork is seriously compromised; failure is almost guaranteed.

The very nature of competition is antithetical to marriage because it's based on proving superiority and defeating your opponent. To "win," competing spouses embrace the thought that "My way is better – it's the right way," Each spouse then sets out to prove the superiority of his or her position. Instead of spouses realizing how they compensate for each other, they undermine each other.

When we feel we're right and our spouses are wrong, we instinctively look for confirmation of our position from others around us. We want our kids, parents, friends, and greater community to see that we're better than our spouses, that we're doing what's best. A sad result of comparing is that it can cause one spouse to give up, drop out, and withdraw. This could lead to living parallel lives.

Additional Information for Step Five A, Withdrawal

Closeness in a relationship tends to run on a spectrum. The following classification may help you assess your current level of closeness.

1. ENGAGED LIVES. Engaged lives means there is almost a constant connection between the couple. The connection may be active one moment and passive the next, but it is constant. (Engaged living is not enmeshed living. Enmeshment is a loss of self into another person, perhaps even to the extent of thinking and feeling that one *is* the other person.)

2. INTERSECTED LIVES. This relationship is characterized by more space and more independent living. The partners join up when they decide to intersect and when outside events create the intersection.

The most common points of intersection in a marriage are:

- Children
- Jobs
- Hobbies
- Religious/spiritual lives and practices
- An issue that a couple decides would be best addressed together

Intersecting couples tend to enjoy or need more space between each other than engaged couples. Or perhaps they feel that they don't have enough in common to live an engaged lifestyle. But they do *look forward* to the times of intersection with each other. Once a couple works out what level of intersection is best for them, or accommodates their individual and joint needs, they can enjoy a thriving relationship.

3. PARALLEL LIVES. Here, independent living defines each of the spouses to such an extent that there is very little intersection. In a parallel marriage, there is coexistence but no real relationship. This can be the result of years of unresolved friction or fighting. Or it can just happen if partners do not communicate and end up growing apart.

Parallel living could also happen as a result of people escaping into their own separate activities of work, sports, internet, television, friends, hobbies, etc. Although these are normally considered life-enhancing activities, the question is proportion. Some people are aware that they're choosing exit routes; others start to slip away unconsciously. Whatever the case, the statement we make in taking any exit route is that "these activities are more important to me than our relationship." Once the relationship takes a back seat to other involvements, the door has been opened to involvement with other people. Although affairs are common at this point, the stage for an affair was already set in the comparing and competing mode.

Sometimes a couple decides to live parallel lives on a conscious level, rather than to divorce. This may be the only valid solution that makes sense to the couple. Howie, a man in our relationship study, chose this route in his marriage, as he revealed in his interview.

HOWIE: My wife and I are married but we don't interact all that much. I mean, I work and she shops...shops...shops...shows me the receipts [sad smile]. Our marriage is a real workshop – I work, she shops. But she has taken good care of our two children. Besides interactions regarding our children, though, I don't have much to say to her. Whenever we do interact, we fight; sometimes it's a contest to see who can scream loudest. Our kids used to try to break it up, but they gave up. Basically, I work, she shops...

CHANA: But you mentioned that you go away on vacations, even now that your kids are grown. Do you interact well on vacation?

HOWIE: Hmm... I wouldn't really call it interaction. She plans the vacation. We travel somewhere together. I go on the guided tours; she runs around shopping. And of course, in every country, we have to have a good fight!

CHANA: So, what keeps you in this marriage?

HOWIE: Well, I would get out. But then again, I'd be so alone if we got divorced.

CHANA: So, there are perks in your marriage?

HOWIE: Yes, I guess so. She makes dinner, there's always someone in the house. I'm more of a passive type of person. She makes sure the house is running... there is always some life in the house. I guess this is worth something. I guess I've gotten used to this and accept that this is as good as it's going to get. I made a conscious decision to stay in the marriage.

4. SEPARATE LIVES. This occurs when the space between the couple is so large that it's defined by avoidance of each other. This is the way Max (another participant in our relationship study) described his marriage, which ultimately ended in divorce: "The relationship turned into nothing; not just no love; it was actually nothing. We had totally separate lives. We lived in separate rooms and didn't even say hello to each other for weeks."

Donna had a similar broken marriage. She and her husband Lee never fought – they never even raised their voices to each other. They had issues, of course, but neither felt comfortable confronting them. "He started to withdraw and do his own thing. So I decided that I'd do the same," Donna relayed. "After that, the marriage just... sort of died."

Most marriages are not fixated in one of these categories; many marriages are in the first or second category (engaged or intersecting) and/or fluctuate between these first two types.

Additional Information for Step Five B, Contempt and Hatred

Resentment, contempt, and hatred damage *us*, not only the person we direct our negativity toward. Hatred is debilitating; it gets in the way of our basic functioning. Instead of dealing with life, people stuck in hatred mode use all of their energy for emotional self-preservation, to stabilize their misery. As they say, hatred is suicide on the installment plan.

Contempt and hatred exacerbate the already existing pressures and stresses that exist in every marriage. In a strong marriage, for example, if the bank calls to announce an overdraft, it is highly stressful but the couple will set out to determine their next move. In a marriage steeped in hatred, the very same call from the bank becomes a showdown. Couples who are working against each other will not have the emotional resources to weather life challenge such as job loss, family tragedy, or financial loss, Nothing has the ability to derail a relationship more than contempt and hatred. If we feel that someone hates us for who we are, we might not even want to solve a crisis together because the relationship is rotting at its core. Issues and struggles will always come up in any marriage, but contempt and hatred are like poison; they make any antidote difficult to administer.

To sum it up, contempt and hatred flow freely when:

- You have a whole story/narrative about what your spouse is doing wrong.
- There is a tendency to habitually tell yourself negative things about your spouse and his/her behavior. By rehearsing these negative thoughts, you actually wire your brain to go into that thought process. You might find yourself putting a negative spin on everything he/she does.
- You forget that your spouse is putting up with your stuff as well. Remember, each one of us is a handful. What is some of your stuff that he/she is putting up with?
- You have totally forgotten all of your spouse's positive traits (gifts) and why you married him/her in the first place.
- You believe the myth that marriage is about getting what you want (which is the fantasy of every child).
- You become addicted to or at least accustomed to the surge of superiority one feels when looking down on someone else.

Appendix C

Personality Typology and This Book

Over the past seventy years, the concept of personality typology has gained tremendous momentum. Although there are many methods of personality typology, the three most influential are Myers-Briggs, Temperament Theory (Keirsey), and the Enneagram. Before I discuss how personality typology relates to my book, here is some basic information about all three of these methods.

Myers-Briggs

Although Carl Jung wrote about personality types in 1920, his book *Personality Types* was relatively unnoticed until the 1950s, when Isabel Myers, a layperson, together with her mother, Kathryn Briggs, discovered this book. They then built their highly influential personality theory, based on Jung's work. Myers and Briggs took Jung's four personality types and developed them into sixteen types. These innovative women then developed the Myers-Briggs

Type Indicator (MBTI), a questionnaire for identifying personality types, which gained tremendous momentum by the 1990s.

Myers-Briggs' sixteen types are:

ISTJ (Introverted Sensing Thinking Judging): quiet, serious, responsible, orderly

ISFJ (Introverted Sensing Feeling Judging): quiet, friendly, responsible, orderly, harmonious

INFJ (Introverted Intuitive Feeling Judging): conscientious, committed, organized, decisive, insightful about people

INTJ (Introverted Intuitive Thinking Judging): original, driven, skeptical, independent, demanding

ISTP (Introverted Sensing Thinking Perceiving): tolerant, flexible, quiet, analytical, efficient

ISFP (Introverted Sensing Feeling Perceiving): quiet, friendly, sensitive, kind, loyal, committed, conflict avoidant

INFP (Introverted Intuitive Feeling Perceiving): idealistic, loyal, curious, quick to see possibilities, adaptable, flexible

INTP (Introverted Intuitive Thinking Perceiving): analytical, theoretical, abstract, quiet, contained, flexible, adaptable, highly focused, skeptical

ESTP (Extroverted Sensing Thinking Perceiving): flexible, tolerant, pragmatic, energetic, spontaneous, tactile

ESFP (Extroverted Sensing Feeling Perceiving): outgoing, friendly, accepting, exuberant, realistic, flexible, spontaneous

ENFP (Extroverted Intuitive Feeling Perceiving): warmly

enthusiastic, imaginative, optimistic, spontaneous, flexible, improvisational

ENTP (Extroverted Intuitive Thinking Perceiving): quick, ingenious, stimulating, alert, outspoken, resourceful, easily bored by routine

ESTJ (Extroverted Sensing Thinking Judging): practical, realistic, matter-of-fact, decisive, organized, systematic, forceful

ESFJ (Extroverted Sensing Feeling Judging): warmhearted, conscientious, cooperative, harmony seeking, loyal

ENFJ (Extroverted Intuitive Feeling Judging): warm, empathetic, responsive, responsible, attuned, loyal, sociable, inspiring leader

ENTJ (Extroverted Intuitive Thinking Judging): frank, decisive, well informed, well read, forceful leader

Temperament Theory

In 1956, psychologist David Keirsey became deeply inspired by the work of Myers and Briggs. However, he did not agree with Myers and Briggs on various points. Keirsey built his four personality types (and subsequent sixteen types) based on the twentieth-century wisdom of Karl Buhler, Kurt Goldstein, Wolfgang Kohler, and others, rather than on Jung. Although Keirsey's work is very similar to Myers-Briggs, there are some fundamental differences. Keirsey's books *Please Understand Me* and *Please Understand Me II* have made a tremendous contribution to the world of personality typology.

Keirsey's sixteen personality types are:

FOUR SPS (ARTISANS)
ESTP (Promoter)
ISTP (Crafter)
ESFP (Performer)
ISFP (Composer)

FOUR SJS (GUARDIANS)
ESTJ (Supervisor)
ISTJ (Inspector)
ESFJ (Provider)
ISFJ (Protector)

FOUR NFS (IDEALISTS)
ENFJ (Teacher)
INFJ (Counselor)
ENFP (Champion)
INFP (Healer)

FOUR NTS (RATIONALS)
ENTJ (Fieldmarshal)
INTJ (Mastermind)
ENTP (Inventor)
INTP (Architect)

The Enneagram

The origin of the Enneagram is under debate. Some say that it dates way back to various teachings from the fourth century. The person who brought the Enneagram to contemporary society is Bolivian-born Oscar Ichazo. In the 1950s, he began his program of self-development which became known as the Enneagram of Personality. The Enneagram is a typology of nine interconnected personality types.

The nine personality types of the Enneagram are:

1. The Reformer: the rational, idealistic type, principled, purposeful, self-controlled, and perfectionistic
2. The Helper: the caring, interpersonal type, demonstrative, generous, people-pleasing, and possessive
3. The Achiever: the success-oriented, pragmatic type, adaptive, excelling, driven, and image-conscious
4. The Individualist: the sensitive, withdrawn type, expressive, dramatic, self-absorbed, and temperamental
5. The Investigator: the intense, cerebral type, perceptive, innovative, secretive, and isolated
6. The Loyalist: the committed, security-oriented type, engaging, responsible, anxious, and suspicious
7. The Enthusiast: the busy, fun-loving type, spontaneous, versatile, distractible, and scattered
8. The Challenger: the powerful, dominating type, self-confident, decisive, willful, and confrontational
9. The Peacemaker: the easygoing, self-effacing type, receptive, reassuring, agreeable, and complacent

How This Book Intersects with Personality Typology

Many people tell me just how much one (or all) of the above methods of personality typology have helped them accept and understand their spouses – and themselves. Yet, many other people express how turned off they are by all of this "personality typing," regarding it as pseudoscientific.

Therefore, in an attempt to reach as many readers as possible, my book relates to "personality traits" rather than personality types. The information and tools in this book are relevant both to those who enjoy personality typology and to those who are not in favor.

One of the benefits and contributions of personality typology is that it normalizes personality differences and promotes the idea that different is not bad. Personality typology has done a tremendous service in helping people break the natural human tendency to relate to a person's personality differences as stupid, crazy, weird, etc.

Because of this, people who are into personality typology might have an easier time avoiding the downward spiral spelled out in chapter 3. However, this does not necessarily translate into these folks having an easier time traveling the upward spiral (chapters 3–9). Although the various systems of personality typology acknowledge that people tend to marry "differences," they do not explain how to live with those differences, day in and day out. This book provides hands-on tools to successfully live and love with your differences.

Along with the above-mentioned benefit of personality typology, there is also an inherent risk. Some people use their "personality type" as an excuse not to grow and change, insisting, "This is just the way I am." Although it is important to honor and accept certain "established" aspects of our personalities, we simultaneously have a tremendous amount of potential for growth and stretching. Self-acceptance does not mean that we stop looking for opportunities for growth and self-expansion. The book you're reading encourages and celebrates this kind of personal growth and personality development.

Over the years, I have met couples who have the following difference to contend with: one partner is into personality typology, while the other partner is not a fan. This can be frustrating to both sides. The pro–personality typology partner strongly desires to share insights and understandings, which often fall on deaf ears. Meanwhile, the skeptical partner not only doesn't share the excitement, but often feels reduced by being defined as a "type." There can also be couples who have the related struggle that one is into the Enneagram, while the other is into Myers-Briggs, so that they both enjoy personality typology but disagree on how to implement it. The good news is that the tools in this book will *also* be helpful for *these* couples to dance with this difference!